Beyond Death

Beyond Death

Empirical Evidence of the Human Soul

by

Timothy Owe

NEW FALCON PUBLICATIONS
TEMPE, ARIZONA, U.S.A.

International Standard Book Number: 1-56184-161-7
Library of Congress Catalog Card Number: 2001093648

First Edition 2003

Cover design by Huphup
http://www.huphup.se

The paper used in this publication meets the minimum requirements of the American National Standard for Permanence of Paper for Printed Library Materials Z39.48-1984

Address all inquiries to:
NEW FALCON PUBLICATIONS
1739 East Broadway Road #1-277
Tempe, AZ 85282 U.S.A.
(or)
320 East Charleston Blvd. #204-286
Las Vegas, NV 89104 U.S.A.

website: http://www.newfalcon.com
email: info@newfalcon.com

Dedicated to the human soul and it's foremost qualities:
generosity, compassion and tolerance.

Empirical (adj) *based on experiment or experience rather than on scientific reasoning*

Evidence (n) *an indication, a ground for belief*

Human (adj) 1. *belonging to mankind as a species;* 2. *having the characteristics of mankind*

Soul (n) 1. *the spirit, a non material part of a person;* 2. *the part of a person that may be expected to survive after death;* 3. *spiritual or emotional force*

— from *The Nelson Contemporary English Dictionary*

TABLE OF CONTENTS

Introduction

W hy prove that we have a soul?
A strange question at first glance, perhaps, as "proving" things is much what human life is about. Why prove that gravity bends light, that the Earth is round, that the sun is the centre of the solar system, for that matter? Well, because when we prove something to a satisfying degree, we treat that something as real. It becomes, at least to us, an inseparable part of reality. Something we must deal with or face the consequences of. Something we cannot ignore. Still, trying to empirically prove that we have a soul, well, that does sound kind of strange. Is that really what science is all about? Is that not something that should be left to theological brooding or the abstract reasoning of philosophers?

Some might feel that attempting to prove the existence of our soul is futile because it is ultimately impossible, because science is irreconcilable with such concepts as the spirit. Others might find the entire endeavour irrelevant as they are already convinced that they have a soul. Yet others may feel apprehensive that science, with its love for defining and categorising, may steal from the mystery of the soul. Perhaps in "dissecting" our inner, eternal being, we will lose something of ourselves. There is truly no telling how people would react to "undeniable scientific evidence" of the soul, especially considering our species' proficiency for full-blown denial.

Still, I think that as a whole, most people would find comfort, whether needed or not, in scientific evidence of spirit. Science and its discoveries do, after all, affect our daily lives to an ever-increasing degree and, as a result of this, influences the way we look at life. If the methods, evidence and logical reasoning of science should prove (or strongly indicate, as is the way of science) that there is a spirit in us that continues to exist beyond death, this should in turn influence science itself and, ultimately, our way of life. In short, such knowledge would change everything.

This is a bold statement to make, as the vast majority of the human population already seems to believe in some sort of a life after death. Most people believe they have a soul of some kind, though naturally there are many versions of what this means. But no matter how much we believe that we have a spirit, most of us believe in the "physical" world to a far greater degree.

Our actions, opinions, thoughts and ambitions almost exclusively concern our lives here and now, whatever we feel will happen beyond death. Looking at the world today where so many of us are homeless, malnourished, subjected to war, illness and greed, where there is so much conflict between individuals, peoples and countries and where we seem completely unable to stop the destruction of our own environment, it seems that this faith is clearly not enough. If we *truly believed* that there was more to life than a few score years, that "we" in some way would continue to exist beyond life on Earth, would we not treat our planet and our fellow inhabitants with more compassion? Would we be able to pursue careers, acquire material wealth, harbour such notions as racism, nationalism and protectionism and turn a blind eye to those less fortunate than us? What would be the point in this, if we *truly believed* we all had a soul that would exist for eternity?

Personally, I believe that if science were to prove that the soul was not only possible but even probable, matters spiritual would eventually move up to the forefront among people's concerns, unlike today when matters material seem to be rewarded with far more attention than those spiritual. Ask yourself the following: if you knew *without any doubt* that what you experience here on Earth is only a portion of what your soul would ultimately experience, and that death is only the end or perhaps the broadening of your temporal personality, would you not lead your life differently?

If I am right about these reactions, then scientific evidence of spirit would be a good thing indeed. But to return to one of the previous objections, is it possible to prove the existence of spirit at all?

First one must remember that it is impossible to prove anything *for certain* in the world of science. A scientific *fact* is merely something that a) has yet to be proved false and b) is very likely to be right. Take gravitation as an example. That an apple will fall to the ground when its attachment to the tree is severed for some reason is considered a scientific fact. There is no reason why it should not, and there is plenty of empirical evidence to back up the assumption that it would. Not only do apples fall to the ground, but oranges, pears, coconuts and any other fruit subjected to the same conditions will do the same. Furthermore, and lending more gravity to the situation as it were, any object that has no reason to be above ground level will fall. People, aeroplanes and meteorites also fall to the ground from time to time. Thus it is a scientific fact that the Earth's gravity will cause things to fall to the ground by drawing things to its centre. But this does not mean that this will always happen. One of these days, an apple might simply stop in midair and just hang there. Just because something behaves a certain way given the same certain conditions a hundred million billion times does not prove that it will do so the next time. It only proves that it behaved so the last hundred million billion trial runs. Still, this seems to be a pretty good foundation to rest upon when making assumptions on future behaviour of apples and gravity, predicting the future being one of the main aims of science from the practical perspective. Or, in other words, this constitutes pretty good proof that the force we call gravity exists, will behave in a predictable way, and should be given considerable practical consideration.

Another significant point is that while we can directly observe apples, people, aeroplanes and meteorites, we can not directly observe gravity, only its effect on us and on other observable objects. Gravity cannot be placed in a test tube or divided into smaller components or in any other way poked, prodded or directly tangibly measured, yet few people doubt that it exists. Actually the same can be said for apples, people, etc. but we shall save this argument for the chapter on consciousness. It is worth noting also that to date no one knows exactly what gravity is, merely how it tends to behave.

So scientific facts are supported by empirical (i.e., observable and tangible) evidence. How then does one go about finding empirical evidence of the soul and its survival after death? Obviously, the soul itself is nothing we can measure directly with instruments or scientific methods. If the soul is to reach the status of scientific fact, it will have to be through the empirical evidence of its effects. To this end we need a hypothesis (such as: "we have a soul that goes on existing after the body dies"), a theory of what the soul is, and ample evidence that the soul does indeed survive beyond death. Any evidence to the contrary must be dealt with and any alternative explanations, however esoteric, must be shown to be less likely than our favoured hypothesis, making the soul the best alternative. And as science (mainly in the guise of classical physics and material reductionism) is traditionally opposed to the notion of the soul, as it is felt that human action can ultimately be explained by genetic and environmental influence, we need also to prove that the classical arguments against the soul are not valid. No simple task, but in the light of the considerable evidence gathered by competent scientists using reliable methods, one I feel (or "consider," as science is supposed to be more rational in arriving at its beliefs than religion) is far from impossible.

At this point I should make clear that this is a book about the results of scientific research and what these results imply. It is not a book *about* scientific research or the protocol such research is conducted under. Though many experiments and studies are referred to and briefly described, for a proper introduction I would advise the readers to go to the various sources I have used. In fact, if you are unfamiliar with research into parapsychology, I recommend that you first acquire a copy of Dean Radin's *The Conscious Universe* (see the "Recommended Reading" chapter for further details) to familiarise yourself with the body of research. This should help most sceptical readers to take a leap of faith long enough to seriously consider the conclusions I propose. If you conclude that the results of said research still remain too outlandish to be taken seriously—as the whole notion of non-local consciousness is simply impossible—then this book will only annoy you further, and little purpose will be served in reading it. On the other hand, if you are prone to accepting anything that seems reasonable without giving adequate sceptical respect to the source, the references to research herein might seem unnecessary and the temptation to browse through it without proper attention might get the better of you. In the interest of expanding mind, (which, next to keeping an open mind, is probably the most important conclusion arrived at in this book), I would recommend reading up on the sceptical perspective. There are several sources on the internet that offer insight on this, and I myself read Michael Shermer's book *Why People Believe Weird Things* (W.H. Freeman and Company, New York, 1997) before embarking on this book.

Though I do not agree with the author in all his conclusions, it is nevertheless a readable and enjoyable introduction to sceptical inquiry, which is a standpoint that almost all of us would benefit from adopting on a more regular basis. As for my own conclusions, that which is empirically demonstrated beyond any reasonable doubt is that which I must build my worldview upon. As I see it, the data or the facts are used to construct the paradigm, and when the facts don't fit the paradigm, it is the latter which must change. I am convinced that the data presented in this book is indeed valid, that there are no flaws in the research serious enough to warrant the discarding of it and, until someone can demonstrate empirically that this data is false, I shall treat it for what it is: very likely to be right.

So exactly how does one go about proving that we have a soul and its (our) continued existence beyond what we call "death"? A brief overview of the line of reasoning is in order.

First, we shall look at what we mean by such concepts as soul or spirit. We need to have a practical definition in order to know what to look for, where to look for it and how to interpret what we find. The definition I have arrived at is *consciousness*. Though I do not equate consciousness with spirit or soul, I believe (as does almost every philosopher throughout history making the similar argument) it is the best link we have to our soul or our true selves. As consciousness, or mind, is a far from fully understood phenomenon, I have also dedicated Chapter 2 for discussion of a few basics. Chapters 3 through 8 deal with different research into the phenomena relevant to our enquiry.

In Chapter 3 we examine whether there is a link between mind and matter, as such a link must be shown if spirit is to be proven. As we shall see, the basic argument against the soul in the wake of Sir Isaac Newton, is that a "non-material" force such as mind, consciousness or spirit should not be able to influence the "material" world. Yet, for there to be any point to the human soul, whatever it is, it must be able to influence the human body. If we fail to prove the mind-matter link, our entire line of reasoning might prove moot. As the logically disposed reader will have already concluded at least the author considers there to be ample proof of such a connection as this book does not finish with Chapter 3.

Having established the crucial mind-matter connection, we will look into the connection between life and consciousness (Chapter

4). In order to do this, we will look into the ancient art of faith-healing as examined in the modern laboratory environment. What is the link between consciousness and life? Is there an animating quality to consciousness which separates living matter from dead? After all, a living body contains exactly same number of atoms as a dead one, the same amount of matter, at least as far as we can tell. What then is the difference between life and death? And if consciousness is that difference, does it remain intact upon leaving its habitat, the body, or does it merely disperse?

Following our discourse into healing and life-force, we shall explore the mind-brain connection in Chapter 5. Is it necessary to have a brain at all to demonstrate a form of consciousness? Here we will examine the evidence of "mental activity" or consciousness in plants and in the cells of animals and humans, neither having neural networks comparable to that of a brain. In conclusion, we shall see that not only is there evidence of consciousness at practically every level in the living organism, but also that a form of communication is taking place that does not require a neural network at all. In fact, a consciousness that does not seem to require any direct connection whatsoever, working independently of time and distance as we recognise it.

These conclusions will lead us back to a re-examination of "non-local consciousness" in Chapter 6. Here more evidence will be presented supporting that we do indeed have access to a form of consciousness that can gather significant information beyond the normal parameters of locality in space and time. Indeed, evidence of a form of consciousness that, at least in a sense, can exist outside of space and time and perhaps even an eternal consciousness, or at least one that might exist beyond death. This raises the question of how death and consciousness are linked together, which is the topic of the next chapter.

Near-death experiences with their out-of-body sensations are the topic of Chapter 7. The notion that mind can separate itself from the body and roam about at will exists in practically every culture, and is practised by both shamans and laymen. Evidence for such a separation of body and consciousness would be very supportive of spirit indeed, and such evidence will be examined here. Of particular interest are such experiences in which corroborative evidence supports the out-of-body experience and cases where the brain is "out cold"; i.e., non-functional. Do these experiences constitute scientific proof that we survive death? Though this stands out as a far more likely alternative to the traditional, materialistic standpoint that consciousness and thus the soul is merely an illusion, it is not the only one. To find conclusive evidence, we must now look for evidence beyond death itself.

The final chapter of empirical evidence (Chapter 8) concerns physical and behavioural evidence of reincarnation. Here we shall see that there are thousands of cases where children seem privy to knowledge of previous lives they could not possibly have acquired in any ordinary way. They also show behavioural traits as well as a strong identification with the previous life. Most significantly, these children are born with birthmarks and birth-defects that correspond to wounds and other physical aspects of the person identified as the previous personality, when such a person can be located. The evidence in this chapter lends further credibility to the survival of consciousness/spirit and presents several challenges against the rival theory of "superpsi."

In Chapter 9 we will construct a hypothesis of what soul/ spirit/consciousness is, and how it relates to life and death, and to the many different accounts of afterlife. Finally, in Chapter 10, we will ask ourselves what it all means, what the purpose of it all is.

Though such philosophical questions and possible answers are both interesting and important, the purpose of the book remains to prove empirically that we have a soul. Again, this does not necessarily have to say more about the true nature of spirit than the falling of apples has to say about the true nature of gravity. I do not believe that we will ever be able to capture a soul in a laboratory test tube but, as I pointed out before, scientific acknowledgement of life beyond death, as unlikely as this may seem at the moment, would most certainly improve the quality and experience of life on Earth.

Scientific method can provide valuable clues to our souls as it uncovers the effects of spirit on the world. If this book should constitute pretty good proof that the force that we have named spirit exists and that spirit might, at least in a sense, have some predictable qualities, perhaps it will be given the same considerable practical consideration as gravity. But if there is anything that has become plain to me during the process of writing this book, it is that we must all uncover our own truths.

Life is, in a very real sense, for learning. The more we learn, the more we will advance in our spiritual voyage. I hope that this book will provide an incitement for all those who give spiritual matters little or no thought in their daily lives to move this activity onto their agenda, into the forefront of their consciousness. I also hope that those readers with a firm idea of what life and the after-life are all about will keep an open mind towards the hypothesis presented here, even if it might not quite correspond to what they believe. This does not mean that my conclusions are correct, merely that considering alternative explanations to one's own is good practice for consciousness. But most of all, I hope that those readers who do not believe they have a soul because this is an *unscientific* notion will see that this is not the case. Because, if the hypothesis presented here proves to be correct, these are the people who will have the most confusing experience as they venture beyond death.

Still, I am a realist and aware of the fact that one single book is not likely to make all that much difference. But once the notion has been presented and the evidence has become common knowledge, a shift in paradigm is inevitable. Such is the nature of scientific curiosity. Progress cannot be stopped and perhaps, for once, this will actually mean real progress.

A hoard of scientists and writers are currently presenting bold new ideas from their various disciplines and areas of expertise and I have not really contributed that much, merely tied their findings together to prove something I think and feel is important. Any praise should go to them, for they, unlike myself, might actually be risking something by researching the areas they are. Without them, and the empirical evidence they have uncovered, this book would not be possible.

Why prove that we have a soul? The proverbial mountain-climber claims to ascend mountains simply because "they are there," and I suppose that, in a sense, it was the same with me. I thought that maybe I could prove we have a soul, given the existing evidence, and once I got that idea into my head I had to at least give it a try. Did I reach the hypothesised peak or lose my scientific balance on some treacherous empirical foothold and fall into a logical crevice along the way? That is for you to decide.

And I promise to steer clear of literary metaphor until we are well past the bewildering path of the evidence.

I

A MATTER OF SPIRIT

We have words and belief. We have words such as *spirit, soul, psyche, self, consciousness* and a thousand more that all denote something that remains somehow beyond the reach of mere words. These are words for something we cannot quite grasp, pinpoint or measure, yet something without which we would not be, or so most of us believe. It is the source of our existence, fundamental to our nature, and the origin of our understanding. Yet we do not understand its nature, even though many of us readily acknowledge its existence.

We cannot measure spirit. It does not lend itself to rulers and scales of contemporary science, and therefore some of us believe that it does not exist at all: that it is a mere illusion arising from the advanced and complicated but nevertheless measurable electrochemical activity of the brain; that it is merely the random evolutionary path of chemistry rising through the laws of physics to a level where it becomes aware of itself and ponders the meaning of it all. Only this and nothing more.

Still, few people can shake the feeling that there is something else, something beyond or within that which can be measured. Few can completely surrender the gnawing suspicion that we are more than atoms forming molecules forming proteins built according to genetic blueprints that have randomly mutated over the ages, for no purpose other than that they just happened to exist in the first place. That the electrochemical switches of the brain are not flicked on and off a billion times each second of their own accord but that something, some force of a different order, is in fact throwing the switches and navigating the brain and body through this thing called life. Absurd, say the defenders of traditional scientific thought. Absurd because it is impossible, because the mind is a result of the body, consciousness is created by the brain, because the evidence clearly states that it is so.

But what if this "hunch" or feeling is correct? What if some kind of spiritual force actually does exists within us. A force that survives the death of our physical body and the subsequent scattering of the atoms which it once was comprised of? And if such a force exists, how should we go about finding it? And how do we prove that what we have found is indeed what we believe it to be, and not just another illusion of our own making created to convince us of something other than the basic futility or pointlessness of existence?

These questions, and many more, we shall have reason to ponder during the course of this book. The foremost problem, however, is that despite most of us having some kind of idea as to what spirit actually is, few of us can provide a clear definition. The definitions that do exist are varied and often too elusive to grasp, let alone use as standards for scientific enquiry. Added to this problem is, as always, the tendency of words to describe sometimes different and sometimes identical things. So, for practical reasons we shall not distinguish between "soul" and "spirit" or other related words. In popular tradition "soul" is often used to denominate a local, human and individual form of spirit, whereas "spirit" is used as a non-local, divine force (as in "Holy Spirit") or in reference to nature as the spirits of animals, places and occurrences such as thunder or rain. If we ever get as far as proving "spiritual energy," we may allow ourselves to indulge in Newtonian distinctions of different forms of spiritual energy, or Aristotelian subgroups of souls, but at this point such distinctions serve little purpose and would probably only confuse our search.

Still, some kind of hypothesis as to what spirit is must be arrived at for this book to serve its purpose. If we do not, we will not know what to look for or indeed know if we have found it. So before we make an attempt at defining it, we should probably review some of the ideas surrounding spirit that science, philosophy and religion has embraced over the ages. Spirit, it turns out, is a far more complicated topic than is usually given credit for.

THE HISTORY OF SPIRIT

There exist a great many creation myths around the world and in most of these some kind of divine spirit is involved. In some myths a divine spirit creates the universe out of nothingness, in others the universe is created out of the divine spirit's body, and in still others the universe is created out of the divine spirit reshaping itself into a new form or forms of tangible spirit. There are many more versions, of course, yet it is these three which concern us most, as they more or less set the parameters of spirituality. Basically, these three types of myths result in three different views on spirituality, which we shall explore presently. Of course, one might also include modern scientific notions of creation here, such as the aptly named Big Bang theory, where the universe just sort of "happened" or was born out of a state unreachable and incomprehensible to us by its very nature. Some scientifically minded people are quite offended by the spiritual implications, favouring the non-spiritual implications of such theories, but as all notions dealing with the creation of the universe deal with the same concept, there is no reason why scientific theories should not be included here. In science, what is held to be mythical and superstitious during one era, might well become the very foundation of the next scientific paradigm. The importance of accepting this possibility will also become evident during the course of our investigation, but for the time being we shall settle for examining the concept of spirit as an idea, not as a reality.

THE BLUEPRINT SOUL

In the first case, the *Great Spirit*, the *Prime Mover*, the *Original Cause*, the *Great Mystery*, *God*, *Allah*, *Yahweh* or the linguistic variation of choice, creates a world out of nothingness. This implies that the world we live in was made *by* God (to opt for the favoured western denomination) but is not *of* God. Therefore the world can be good, evil, a little of both or neither. Genesis, the creation myth of the Bible, is an excellent example of such a myth. God creates the world out of nothingness, populating it finally with humans created in God's image. Nowhere in this myth is it clearly stated that the world or the humans are "a part of God," leaving the nature of the world, as well as the human spirit, open to interpretation. Needless to say, this has resulted in its fair share of controversy over the years. Some Christian sects, such as the Gnostics, opted for the world being basically an evil place and physicality something one should strive away from in order to reach God. Other sects came to regard the world as their birthright, and therefore something that they were free to use or abuse as they saw fit. Still others saw the world as a manifestation of God, and thus something to be treated with respect. In most cases, however, the theme was (and perhaps still is) one of separateness. God and divinity was elsewhere, man and the world here.

To create an analogy for this view, imagine an anthill as representing the world with the ants representing the humans. God, in this case, would be the distinguished elderly and bearded gentleman standing beside the anthill in his robes, and observing the activity (sternly or fondly, depending on your religious orientation). The ants (i.e., we humans) have no possibility of understanding the man (i.e., God), his nature or his actions. If he chooses to poke a stick into the anthill and twirl it about, we will understand that something has happened, but will have no way of understanding what actually took place. God and the mysterious ways in which God operates are something we cannot comprehend, as God is infinitely superior and ultimately separate from us. Not a very encompassing analogy perhaps, or very flattering to us ants, but hopefully it will serve its purpose without offending too many readers.

A second, and in this case more important, aspect of this separateness is the spiritual one. If humans are created out of ultimate "nothingness" (albeit in God's image), do they have a soul, a spark of divinity? Though most Christians, Jews and Muslims subscribing to the Old Testament probably assume they have a soul of sorts, it is interesting to note that apparently nowhere does this particular document specifically state that this is the case. The resurrection theme is very much a physical or bodily one, where the souls of the righteous upon judgement day shall be resurrected into an implied physical state. Even the resurrection promised in the New Testament is one similar to that of Christ, i.e., of a physical nature.

The soul in this particular version is simply a "blueprint" of the person. Upon the death of the individual, the blueprint is archived away to await judgement day. Only at this point in time will the good and evil be resurrected and judged. Among modern Christian movements, the Jehovah's Witnesses are an example of diligent adherents to this version, believing firmly that the date is close at hand, and working hard at saving as many souls as possible before the final day of judgement and subsequent resurrection.

Of course, Christianity is far too diverse a religion for all or even most major sects to agree with this view of the soul. Indeed, it would seem that most denominations regard heaven and the afterlife as a spiritual place rather than a physical one, and human life as at least partly divine or holy. That the human soul indeed contained a spark of divinity might well have been the point of view originally preached by Christ himself, if one is to believe the Gnostic texts and gospels of Thomas.

Leaving the various interpretations of Christianity aside, we have here at least one view of the soul: the blueprint that continues to exist after the death of the physical body, but only in an inanimate form. The blueprint soul has no life or even substance of its own, but plays a highly significant role at the day of resurrection and judgement. The view is rooted in a creation myth that separates that which God has created from God "himself," and stipulates that man means nothing, has come from dust and is likely to return to dust, but can aspire to something by serving God through doing God's will. Man exists because it pleases God.

THE HUMAN SOUL

In another version of creation, God sacrifices his divine being to create the world. The body then becomes the world, which we live in and consist of. Actually, in most such cases, it is a feminine divinity in the guise of a Goddess who gives birth to the world, or creates the world from her own body. This should not come as a surprise as this merely echoes what human females have done since the first specimen of our species, only on a greater, more celestial scale. Here spirituality and physicality become naturally linked to each other.

Most of the world's "less" developed people subscribe to this view, as did/does the Pagan movement, the dominant religion in Europe before Christianity. Spirit holds a fundamental position here and the spirit world is regarded to be as real as the physical world, sometimes even more so. Each individual has a spirit, but so does each animal, each plant, each place, each happening and so on. The interconnectedness among all things is emphasised, and man's position is more humble as the Earth itself is God. Man is not given the Earth to do with as he pleases, but to be a part of and to respect. We are the children of the Earth, not its masters.

Upon death, the body is returned to the cycle of nature, but often the spirit remains intact and active, taking on slightly supernatural qualities. The spirit becomes an ancestor, retaining at least its personality if not its physicality or its proximity, and continues to live in the spiritual dimension. As pointed out, this dimension is strongly linked to the physical world and occasionally ancestors will, if called upon, breach the wall between the two in order to help out in the physical. A good spirit can also be counted on to assist against unfriendly spirits. Enemies in life might well go on to be enemies in death, so there is no reason to believe that the fundamental rivalry and strife connected with life should cease to exist just because one takes on a spiritual form. In any case, death is a mere transition, and the spirit along with its unique personality remains active. In some versions spirits remain in the spiritual, in others reincarnation is the expected practice.

To return to the analogy of the anthill, God no longer is the bearded man on the sideline, but rather the anthill itself (which becomes a living thing) and, to a certain extent, the ants. The purpose of life resulting from this perspective becomes more diverse. We do not exist for God's amusement or because of God's will as such, but rather we are a manifestation of the divine, albeit to a small degree, as is everything else. Obviously there is still a spiritual purpose to life, and though it differs from interpretation to interpretation, it usually is concerned with living in harmony with nature and doing "the right thing," as it were. The latter becomes especially important in cases of reincarnation, but even as one moves on into the world of spirits one brings along only the qualities one developed in life. The mighty warrior remains the mighty warrior and the coward remains the coward, or so it would seem.

Though more advanced as far as spiritual autonomy is concerned than the previous myth, which offered little more than more of the same at a later date, this myth is still fairly simple. There is one physical world and there is one spiritual world, and that is pretty much it. You go from one to the other or perhaps recycle between them, but basically there are only two dimensions to reality.

The Extended Soul

In the third kind of creation myth, the divine being creates the world out of a portion of this divinity, thus remaining whole, or at least partially intact. Though the world is a physical place the focus remains on the spiritual, as the spiritual is in essence the same divine matter that is God. In other words, we are all a portion of God, all united by a shared divinity. In this view the world is a real enough place, but exists mainly as a breeding or training ground for the spirit, the purpose of the world being to test or develop spirits in one way or another. Reality, as we recognise it, is what Plato would have referred to as "the world of shadows." Reality is real in the sense that we, our emotions and thoughts, are real, but there is a more fundamental reality beyond or within this one. This does not mean that the physical world is not real, the world has spirit also, and therefore is equally real. But as we leave this world, we find that our spirit is far greater than the limited version we had to rely upon while we were experiencing life as human beings on Earth.

Though this concept is most deeply rooted in the diverse movement collectively named "New Age", aspects of it do occur in more ancient cultures. In Native American tradition, for example, the Great Spirit sends little portions of itself (us) to Earth Mother in order for them to experience life and all the problems of the physical world. Through this work the little spirit grows, so that upon returning to the Source, Great Spirit becomes even larger. Our true home is with the Great Spirit, but Earth is our home away from home, and all things have a spiritual aspect. Other versions state that our Earth is the most physical planet of the universe to which souls from all over the universe come to learn about physicality. Another common theme is Earth as the only place where total free will exists, having been created as a "free will experiment." In this cosmology Earth is but the most dense (physical) level of existence, that ranges from physicality to pure spirit (Prime Cause or God) with many layers on the way. Life on Earth is only one of the many forms of life that the spirit may experience. The variations of this theme seem endless, but basically human existence on Earth is seen as only one of many different forms of existence available for our spirits.

Whether this notion be true or not, it is still significantly different from most traditional religious doctrines that tend to take on a very human-centred and dichotomised view of the world. The spiritual universe is no longer divided into being alive with the option of an afterlife (or possibly the mutually exclusive options of Heaven and Hell), nor is the spirit basically human in nature. Indeed, the thought that upon death we might find ourselves to be far greater entities than we could have imagined during life, and that we have much living in other dimensions and realities left before we may return to God, is one few people would seem to have seriously pondered.

Applying this view onto our anthill analogy, God would be the elderly gentleman (or rather not an elderly gentleman at all, but as pointed out earlier this is a limited analogy) as well as the ants and the anthill. No division would exist among them other than that of perspective and possibly spiritual growth or objective. There would also be lots of other anthills of shapes and sizes different from "our" hill, representing different universes, dimensions or other "places" where spirit might reside. In contrast to the first case, we find ourselves small portions of God, yet we are not God any more than an atom or any other single aspect of our body is us, though it is a part of us.

The three views of the human spirit or soul so far are therefore:

- The blueprint in need of a physical body to exist.
- The soul that leaves the body upon death yet remains pretty much human, though incorporeal, without a physical body.
- The soul which is only partly human to begin with, and that goes on to new forms of existence after physical death.

Naturally these definitions are bound to blend with each other. A typical case is that of reincarnation, a view that deserves some extra consideration.

RECYCLED SOULS

Reincarnation is basically a case of spiritual recycling, and as always with recycling there are two ways to go about it. In the one case the recycled product is returned to the market in its original shape, as for instance a glass bottle. In the other the product is returned to the market after being processed into a new shape, as with paper, where it is shredded and mixed with other recycled material as well as new pulp.

The common interpretation of reincarnation usually consists of the following cycle: the soul becomes one with the physical body at some time between conception and birth. The human, being now both body and soul, goes through life hopefully attempting to do more good than bad and eventually passes on. The spirit is then judged according to the laws of karma, and if it has behaved well it returns to life better off than the last time. Eventually, after going through this cycle a number of times, the soul will be united with the Source, a state of perpetual bliss and divinity.

In a sense, the soul is like a cube of sugar and the body is like its wrapping paper. The sugar cube represents the soul and the wrapping represents the body. After a completed life, the wrapping is shed and the sugar cube returns to the spiritual sugar bowl, to lie in wait with the other sugar cubes for its next rightfully earned wrapping. Here the cube or spirit remains more or less the same in essence, perhaps growing slightly more refined or true to its spiritual nature, though the body varies from life to life. With every new life, spirit creates a new personality from scratch (if this is indeed how personality is created). This personality, with its emotions and memories, must ultimately be discarded with its accompanying body and the actions taken by it weighed on the karmic scales in the spiritual. Before the next designated life can be embarked upon, all spiritual recollection of previous lives must be hidden from the conscious mind. If this were not the case, each life would become gradually more confusing. Imagine if you will, returning to the world as the daughter to a person whose grandfather you were in the previous life. A quite possible outcome, if one is to believe this particular model of reincarnation.

The motivator or force behind the wheel of reincarnation is generally karma in the sense of justice. In the current life you pay the dues or reap the benefits of the previous life. The political implications are obvious, implying that the upper classes are better off because it is the will of God or the universe, but the notion of karma is subtler than this, existing not only between lives but also during them. As the saying states: what comes around, goes around.

The notion that one can be affected by previous lives beyond pure setting postulated by karma is no stranger in reincarnation circles. Reincarnation circles are pretty big, by the way, as a majority of the world's population subscribes to this idea in one way or another. Past life memories are now being researched by scientists, and there exists a fair amount of biological evidence in favour of reincarnation that we shall examine in a later chapter. But, in any case, questions concerning "personal identity" in relation to "spiritual identity" become rather tricky to answer, since each individual lifetime is no more than a temporal identity, necessary to develop spirit. The quality of spirit developed then defines the circumstances of the next life and its accompanying identity. Depending on what happens on the "other side," this temporal identity might serve as anything from a blueprint to an extended self, as mentioned earlier. One cannot help but wonder which personality is dominant between lives. Perhaps one develops a composite personality based on all of one's previous lives, much as we in this life mould our different traits and internal conflicts into one personality. Perhaps something entirely different.

To complicate things further, we have soul recycling in the terms of pulp. Imagine, if you will, spirit as loose sugar rather than a definite cube. After life ends and the wrapping paper is discarded, the sugar is returned to the bowl. In order for a new life to commence, the celestial teaspoon is dipped into the sugar bowl and the content is poured into the new wrapping paper.[1] Thus, each person living on Earth has a spirit consisting of fragments of those that have lived before. On a humorous note, this would explain why so many people believe they were Julius Caesar, Cleopatra or Napoleon in a previous life, as this in part may be true. If we are to apply contemporary scientific paradigms to the soul, this makes sense too. After all, if the body consists of atoms that are replaced over time, then why not the soul? The Greek philosopher Democritus himself, who originally came up with the notion of atoms (*atomos*—that which cannot be divided), proposed that the soul consisted of a specific kind of spiritual atom. From a holistic standpoint it also makes sense, tying spirit into everything else in one common and interrelated reality.

From the individual perspective, the notion of our spirits being mixed together is, perhaps, the most difficult aspect to embrace. Imagine the "you" in you to be as eternal as the atoms that your body consists of, yet as fickle, interchangeable and impersonal as these atoms. We humans are by the very nature of our perceptions forced into an individual approach to the world, and naturally this approach also affects our view of the afterworld.

Spirits Great and Small

"Size doesn't matter," is a popular saying in our society. It is, however, not true. We live in a physical world, and size is therefore of some consequence. Try tightening a bolt with a wrench that is just slightly the wrong size, if you are in any doubt about this. Spirit, on the other hand, is not physical by nature, and therefore little serious thought is given to its size. It is simply politically correct to assume that everyone has the same amount of spirit. Well, what if we don't?

Some philosophers argue that man is born without a soul, acquiring one through living. The potential is there, but how much or how little we create is really up to us. Thus, the more spiritual a life lived, the more spirit. This concept that spirits could be large and small, or better and worse, should perhaps not come as a surprise. Most organised religions emphasise certain conduct in humans to make the celestial cut, implying that some behaviour is more in line with spiritual growth or good karma than other behaviour. The reward of earthly sacrifice is supposed to come in heaven (for pious Christians) or in a better subsequent life (for pious Hindus), though the risk of hellfire and poverty may well have been even more compelling motivators in the past. Clearly God or the Divine Force was not supposed to treat all souls equally, rewarding them without thought as to how they had lived their lives. Some judgement was to be measured out, and though this may be done in reference to actions taken or not taken during life, it seems that these actions inevitably affected the soul. It is, after all, the soul and not the body that has to face judgement in the afterlife, even when this is only a case of possible re-animation. So it is generally supposed that some souls are worthier than others, that some souls are of a better quality or are simply larger than others, in the sense of containing "more of the good stuff." Some may be better off at the start of life on Earth than others, as with reincarnation, but in most cases the quality of the soul and its destiny after life on Earth is firmly moulded *during* life on Earth.

Ironically, it was supposedly this deep concern for the "immortal soul" and its well-being that sparked the Spanish Inquisition and subsequent centuries of witch-burning in medieval Europe. By confessing one's sins, one would salvage one's soul from eternal hellfire. One's body had to be forfeited though, often by fire and after a great deal of torture, but that was just how the cookie, or perhaps oblate, crumbled in those days. The Catholic Church has actually got a slightly worse rap than it deserves, at least in Protestant cultures, when it comes to witch-burning. Apparently the cases that got as far as a proper church trial usually ended more favourably for the "witch" than those that began and ended with the volatile mass-psychosis acted by self-righteous mobs in town squares. The tales of what humans are prepared to do to each other and themselves in order to save or improve their souls or their lives range from the frightening to the fascinating, but this is beside the point. The qualities and causes that define a great spirit from a small one may have some relevance though.

There are many examples, both contemporary and historical, of people who, we might argue, seem to be great souls—people we admire and turn to for advice, insight and inspiration. On the other end of the scale, there are many people we might hold up as "deterring" examples—people who we feel are, if not evil, then certainly sad excuses for human beings. The various qualities we connect with these individuals may differ from person to person, but most of us can make a list of qualities we regard as more spiritually desirable than others. Which of these qualities we ourselves choose to pursue, incorporate or develop in our beings are another matter entirely, but how free are we to do this? We can look to those who we admire both most and least and ask ourselves if their lives and personalities might not have turned out completely different, had not fate treated them differently. Indeed, we might well ask ourselves how much of our own lives do we actually shape, and how much does the cause-and-effect nature of destiny shape for us? Or, do we somehow choose our own destiny before we are born? These are issues that we shall perhaps never fully understand, but they do raise the interesting and philosophically significant question of how much responsibility one actually has for one's own actions.

SPIRIT AND FREE WILL

Free will seems to be the central issue in the battle between science and religion. Newton himself may have been a religious man with esoteric interests ranging as far as alchemy, but his laws certainly did not leave much room for free will, when drawn to their inevitable conclusion. Causality does not make much allowance for free will, but free will is crucial for the soul. If the soul is not free to act out its own will, how can it chose "the right path" or use its tenure on Earth to develop itself? Could spirit exist without free will and for what purpose then?

The issue of free will has been probed and pondered by both scientists and clergy alike. From a scientific pre-quantum perspective, the issue of free will seldom causes much conflict on a practical level. It is an interesting concept, one studied especially by artificial intelligence engineers and marketing professionals, but remains a question for speculative philosophers rather than empirical scientists. In the traditional view, the billiard balls of our mind are not continuously poked with divine or spiritual cues but were merely set into motion some 15 billion years ago, and will continue to collide in a predictable manner until the table finally collapses into itself. Causality really leaves no room for free will at all, and if you catch yourself wondering why things were set in motion with the big bang all those years ago, well, join the rest of the world's theoretical physicists.

For religion, free will proves to be more of a double-edged sword. If it exists, then man can act against the will of God, which implies that God is not almighty. If it does not exist, then man's actions ought to be absolved as man ultimately is not responsible. To the best of my knowledge, the theological jury is still out on that one.

In pre-Christian Greece it was a common religious theme that man was born with a destiny, and thus had no real free will, other than, perhaps, the choice of which path to follow to the preordained destination. In the play "Oedipus", the father is informed that his child is destined to kill him and wed his wife, the child's mother. In an attempt to avoid this destiny, the royal father has a trusted subject place the child in the woods to be devoured by wolves, but the trusted subject takes pity on the child and raises him as his own. Eventually the child does slay his biological father and wed his mother, as is his destiny, and it all ends with the usual wailing, mutilation and self-loathing despair of the average upbeat Greek tragedy. The essence is not what Freud later suggested, but that man should not attempt to meddle with destiny as decreed by the gods. On the other hand, this apparently did not stop the Greeks from appealing to the gods of Olympus to intervene on their part, which the gods apparently did on occasions when it suited them, so perhaps the ancient Greeks were allowed to use some portion of free will to argue their case with the Gods. Considering how complicated the issue of free will actually is, it is not surprising that the Greeks churned out so many interesting philosophers.

The concept of Karma, an integral part of Buddhism and Hinduism, stipulates that humans have free will but that it comes with a price. The law of karma is roughly "what goes around, comes around" as the choices you make and the actions you take all result in counter actions later on that may or may not be beneficial to you. This law gives you what you have coming, be it good or bad, in this life or in the next, without exceptions or courts of appeal. Interestingly though, karma is a divine law rather than a divine being. It exists as a dynamic natural law of the spirit, rather than a godlike entity passing judgement after a particular set of rules. The notion of a natural way of all things can be found in Taoism also. This is in fact central to the Tao ("the Way"), and as one can act both against and along with what is natural, individual free will is implied here also. Yet Taoists also claim that the Tao is inevitable, that it will ultimately have its way, which in turn implies that free will cannot go against the Tao in the long run. The actual oneness of this seeming dualism is represented in the two waves creating the one symbol of the Tao.

Astrology, at times rejected and at times embraced by Christianity, is another case where free will, determinism and God meet. It was originally attacked by the Church Fathers on the grounds that it was a form of divination, and as such condemned by the Old Testament. The implication that man's actions were ruled by the stars and not by man himself obviously made the whole point of salvation meaningless. Astrology remained popular, however, and eventually theologians managed to reconcile the conflict by stating that astrology could affect the physical aspects of man but not the spiritual ones. The stars could, for instance, predict illness and suggest cures, but could not dictate the actions of the individual soul. When astrological forecasts proved to be true, this was held as evidence that the spirit was often weaker than the flesh and thus succumbed to its pleasures and desires. This attempt to reconcile astrology and Christianity was first put forward by none other than the reformer Thomas of Aquinas, and the issue of spirit, free will and body is as relevant today as it ever was. Most of us have done things we know we probably should not have done, things that the body desired rather than the spirit. It would seem that bodily needs and desires are one of the greatest challenges of the spirit and the battleground where free will is most likely to be wielded, providing that such a thing exists in the first place. Obviously someone who is physically or mentally addicted to something is going to need to conjure up far more willpower when it comes to kicking the habit than someone who is not. So does this mean that addictions are good for the spirit, as long as we conquer them rather than succumb to them? Is life all about dealing with different kinds of physical addictions in an effort to free the soul from its status as a "life junky," as it were?

Many people would probably agree that the less free will you have, the less life or spirit you have, but even the standpoint that free will is necessary to spirit is debated. Angels, for instance, are said to be spirits that have surrendered their free will completely to God according to some Christian traditions. Lacking free will, however, in no way denies them spirit or consciousness. On the contrary, angels are seen as great spiritual presences by many people today, as literature, seminars and workshops on angelic issues remain a popular feature within the realm of New Age.

Conscious Spirit

Perhaps, then, consciousness or awareness is the sole trait that cannot be separated from spirit. This would seem to be a reasonable departure point as we search for evidence of the soul. Philosopher René Descartes' statement *cogito, ergo sum* (I think, therefore I am) is one of the most widely quoted and fundamental philosophical statements ever to be made, delving into the very nature of reality as it does. Though the definition of "I" and the meaning of "think" and "exist" will invariably differ from individual to individual, the sentiment expressed remains the same. Consciousness would seem to stand out as the only spiritual aspect that remains constant in all spiritual teachings. This consciousness may vary, from retaining an individual perspective in Christian belief, to losing its individuality through becoming one with all that is in Buddhism, yet it remains consciousness. Even the atheist will usually accept consciousness as evidence of existence, though is likely to argue that consciousness is merely a spin-off product of the physical world. Hopefully, even those subscribing to this point of view might experience a change of mind (or heart, as our beliefs unfortunately tend to rest on faith rather than fact), if this consciousness, this "I think," can indeed be shown capable of existing without a living body to sustain it. Is the human being merely an advanced biological machine, built by atoms to perpetuate genes and perhaps to serve as a host for bacteria, or are human bodies physical containers of a spirit that lives on beyond these bodies inevitable demise? This, then, is the question.

SUMMARY

Spirit, as we have seen, is a far more complicated issue than usually given credit for. Is it an illusion or a blueprint, does it visit the Earth once or return several times, does it start out as a spark and grow, or is it far larger than we can possibly comprehend with our limited brains, only a fraction of it inhabiting the physical body? Intriguing though these issues are, until the existence of spirit itself has been indicated they remain premature. But to prove its existence we must define some basic and inseparable feature for which to search.

The only feature compatible with all the above versions of spirit, yet which neither favours nor denies one, is consciousness. Consciousness is the Cartesian *sum* of existence, no matter what form it may take. Thus, if we can prove that consciousness continues to exist after the body and brain have ceased to function, we will have proven that spirit exists.

The aim of this book is therefore to find empirical evidence that consciousness survives the body after it is irrevocably dead. Before we examine the evidence, however, we need to make one further stop. We need to examine the nature of consciousness itself.

II

CONSCIOUSNESS

C onsciousness, then, is the link to our soul, our indication of spirit. At first glance this may seem like a simple and fairly straightforward statement, but as always there are finer points to be made and objections to be raised. And, as always, when using such abstract concepts as "consciousness," the field of interpretation is wide.

Though consciousness has many measurable aspects which have been poked and prodded and tested by practically every scientific discipline at one time or another, the true nature of consciousness remains an issue of speculation. Much of this book will be dedicated towards examining little-known yet thoroughly and meticulously researched aspects of consciousness that might tell us a thing or two about this nature, or at least tell us something about what consciousness is not. Nevertheless, before we take the plunge into this highly significant material a few words on the more traditional views of consciousness are in order. If we are to go about looking for evidence of consciousness surviving the death of the brain, we had better have a fairly clear idea of what we are searching for.

THE HISTORY OF CONSCIOUSNESS

Throughout history, research and speculation into the nature of consciousness has been an issue of some concern. Every half-decent philosopher concerned with the nature of the way things are, or at least the way things appeared to be, inevitably had to take a stab at defining consciousness.

Socrates, commonly regarded as the first great western philosopher, concluded that he knew only one thing, and that was that he knew nothing. Some might argue, from a logical point of view, that this is a contradiction. After all, if one knows that one knows nothing, then one knows something, which means that one doesn't know "nothing" at all. Despite the double negations and the apparent contradictions of Socrates' conclusion, it says something very significant about human consciousness and something we all would do well to remember: human consciousness is clearly a limited thing. These limitations are by no means the sole discovery of Socrates, but are the basis of most mystical schools of thought over the world. Mystics still attempt to get past the limitations of consciousness using everything from artificial drugs to pure meditation, but their findings rarely translate well into normal consciousness, and are commonly explained away by said normal consciousness as mere delusions. We will have reason to revisit some of this evidence in the final chapters of this book, but as it is anecdotal rather than empirical, it serves no purpose in our search for evidence.

The most important historical figure for our line of reasoning is not to be found in ancient Greece but in France, some 400 years ago. As mentioned in the previous chapter, René Descartes, or Cartesius as he was known in the more fashionable Latin, came to a rather significant conclusion regarding consciousness. Descartes realised, much like Socrates, that there was no sure knowledge in the world. No contemporary philosophies, religious or secular, could offer a scrap of evidence in support of their own validity. So Descartes decided to mull over the subject of philosophy in order to find one true, undeniable statement, thought or fact on which to build an entirely new and reliable philosophy. What he came up with were the famed words *cogito, ergo sum* (Latin) roughly meaning *consciousness, thus existence.* Or, more simply put: "I think, therefore I am." The only argument to be made against this was: "You only think you are thinking," which could easily be countered with: "Who in that case is doing the thinking?" It seems that the "I" can be, and usually is, brought under suspicion, but that is about it.

Descartes further divided the world into two different parts, *res cogitans* and *res extensa.* The former refers to our "inner" world—the realm of cognition, thought and sensation—whereas the latter means "that which is extended in space"—the material world. In a sense: the spiritual and the material. Where the material was confined to time and space, the spiritual, argued Descartes, was not. This has later become known in philosophical circles as Cartesian duality, and the link between these two worlds was one Descartes unfortunately failed to address either to his own or anyone else's satisfaction. Though few people at the time questioned the reality of the spiritual, the failure to come up with a clear connection between this and the equally believable material world, would in time prove to have dire consequences for the champions of spirit in their war against the champions of science and rationality.

Operating at the same time in England was Isaac Newton, an equally brilliant thinker. Though Newton himself was a firm believer in the divine, his greatest accomplishments were in explaining the workings of the material world through mathematics. Though his laws of motion and gravity failed to account for the exact paths of the heavenly bodies, they were a very good approximation that would not be improved upon until centuries later by another brilliant thinker, Albert Einstein. Newton explained the slight discrepancies between his mathematical equations and the actual behaviour of the planets through Divine Intervention. God apparently nudged the planets once in a while, just to keep them on track, claimed Newton. Naturally, Newton was not without his critics, who felt that the "invisible arm" (gravity) seemed a little too esoteric and mystical an explanation of why planets circled the sun and people did not simply spin off the Earth due to centrifugal force. Still, whatever it was, gravity seemed to work, and nowadays few scientists seem to have any trouble accepting this or any other forces of nature that are not observable to the eye, as long as they behave in a mathematically reliable way.

Ironically, when combining the insights of Descartes and Newton—both believers in God and spirit—the notion of spirit (and God) seems to fare all the worse. If spirit, which according to Descartes is a non-material force, was to influence the material world, non-material forces must be able to influence material forces. Yet the laws of Newton clearly stated that only material forces could influence material forces. The logical conclusion would be that spirit cannot influence our body (or the actions of our body, or the way electric charges behave within the neurones of our brain), let alone any other physical object or process. And if spirit cannot influence, what could possibly be the purpose of its existence? To observe, one might argue, but the more science developed along the path of reductionism, the less credibility this argument received.

Though the discovery of energy fields, such as magnetism, compelled many an animist to argue that everything was alive and infused with spirit, the overall path of science seemed selected. Along that path consciousness became less an expression of spirit and more an expression of a natural process, a result of brain activity, an epiphenomenon with no "substance" of its own. Humanity's spiritual nature received another blow from Darwin's theory of natural selection, stipulating that we were no more than advanced animals who had basically reached this level due to the beneficial qualities of random mutation. True, we were favoured in a sense, perhaps, but hardly of the spiritual proportions that being favoured over all others by God suggested. The laws of chance and circumstance came to explain the creation of man, not the laws or interventions of God. Later, Freud dove into the human mind, the last bastion of spirituality, and demonstrated that it too operated under certain laws, laws which became the objective of psychology to uncover. In the eyes of many scientists, consciousness became little more than a delusion. Research into computers and other information processing systems seemed to come up with similarities to the human brain, leading many a researcher to claim that the mind was no more than a highly advanced biological computer. So, within a matter of a century or two, the learned view of consciousness went from something divine to something mechanical.

But as always with the progresses and refinement of scientific method and its accompanying glimpses into deeper levels of the material world, a new view emerges. Looking inside cells, a complexity is revealed that goes far beyond anything that random mutation could explain, microbiologists argue.[1] And peering inside atoms, a world is revealed that is impossible to understand in Newtonian terms of predictable laws, a world where time and distance do not exist as we understand them, yet a world which "our" world consists of.

Speculation in the wake of quantum physics is fascinating, particularly when concerning consciousness, and though many dignified physicists have argued for a mystical view of the world,[2] this is nothing we can lean upon. We have little use of speculation since we must rely on facts arrived at through empirical research. Such facts, fortunately, exist in ample degree, as we shall see later, but for now let us acquaint ourselves with the two competing views of consciousness.

What Is Consciousness? (Part I)

The number of scientific papers concerning the nature of consciousness is anyone's guess. Psychologists, biologists, neurologists, zoologists, information scientists, not to mention artists, poets, theologians and philosophers—in short representatives from practically every scientific, religious and cultural walk of life—have taken a stab at it. Yet the true nature of consciousness remains a mystery. No one really knows how it works, let alone what it is. This is partly due to the fact that everyone studying consciousness does so from a particular perspective, thus uncovering certain aspects rather than addressing the phenomenon as a whole.

The dominant contemporary view is that consciousness is a mere illusion, a spin-off effect of the advanced biological computer we recognise as our brain. The organism receives information through the normal senses, and while processing this information in order to act upon it in the most beneficial way for the organism, we get the impression that we are individuals thinking thoughts, making decisions and taking more or less resolute action. *Thoughts are to the brain what urine is to the kidneys*, stated 19th century zoologist Karl Vogt, with pointed elegance. In other words, consciousness is merely a waste-product of the brain's natural and completely different purpose. We might think we are thinking our thoughts, but in actual fact it is our thoughts that are "thinking" us. Confusing, yes, but no doubt a valid point. The fact that an illusion is extremely convincing does not make it reality, merely a very good illusion, retainers of this point of view would argue.

Of course, one might argue, this demands a reason for the illusion to have developed in the first place. After all, this perspective is closely related to Darwinism, which states that every feature in nature exists for a reason in that it benefits the organism in some way or another. If it did not, it would merely demand space and resources that could be used for something else that would serve an actual purpose. So what possible purpose might the illusion of consciousness serve? Consciousness, or the sense that "we" are actually influencing our own thoughts and lives, is not actually necessary for "us" to live our lives, according to this view. Clearly there is no such purpose. We would be perfectly happy going through the motions of life like good little computers without any clue that we actually existed and performed functions in the physical world. But, on the other hand, if consciousness is an illusion, then it does not really exist at all. And if it does not exist, it does not have to meet any scientific requirements. Consciousness is inevitable, one might argue, as any sensory process resulting in mental decisions leading to actions will have to register in some way. So consciousness exists in a very lowly way in the simple amoeba, reaching its peak with the complex wiring of the human brain. Perhaps computers experience some kind of consciousness too. How would we know?

The above back-and-forth reasoning does not actually prove anything, as it is a mere hypothetical argument. If consciousness is an illusion, what is to say that anything we try to understand or explain by use of consciousness is anything but an illusion?

In a sense, everything is an illusion because, though we may experience an outside world of people, trees, cars, the sea, bagels, love songs and television, these all exist only in our head. Or rather, our interpretation of them exists only in our head. Another influential philosopher, Immanuel Kant, pointed out that we can have no knowledge of the outside world—the object in itself *(das ting an sich)*—but only of our perception of that object. "Object" is to be interpreted as anything and everything existing in the outside world within the coordinates of time and space, *res extensa*. Kant also claimed that the human mind experiences the world in specific ways, which is interesting to note as this allows us a certain level of shared knowledge of the outside world. Our inability to prove that the outside world exists has never been successfully challenged by any philosopher, but this does not appear to bother anyone. Our minds seem quite content to operate under the assumption that if it looks real, feels real and smells real, it probably *is* real—even if it isn't.

The second point of view is, of course, that consciousness is not an illusion at all but something *actual*, something that exists on its own, something that is real and ultimately independent of the brain. The variations of this theme are many but in most cases the brain is given at least some credit as the instrument through which consciousness translates and interacts with the physical world. A human is, simply put, more than the sum of her physical parts. As the inspired romantics pointed out in opposition to the champions of the age of reason: we can place a human on the scales, measure her height and weight, but this tells us nothing of her nature.

The versions and implications of this standpoint are as noted diverse to say the least, but a rising number of scientists from different disciplines seem to be embracing this perspective. This is good news for us, as the previous perspective leaves no room for such "quaint" notions as the soul. This understanding of consciousness allows for a very different interaction with the physical world, as well as a different origin. Where consciousness has no real purpose or meaning in the earlier reductionist or materialist version, the opposite is true here. Ultimately, it is consciousness that gives reality (i.e., the material world) meaning, as reality without anything capable of experiencing it would be quite pointless. Indeed, some would argue that it is consciousness that gives substance its "substance," as opposed to the other way around.[3]

This last assumption raises the question of the limits of consciousness. Are all things conscious, or merely humans and the other mammals followed by other animals to a lesser degree? Does a lake, a grove or a single oak have consciousness or spirit as many a pagan, aborigine or other animist would claim? Do quarks and electrons display basic properties of consciousness as some quantum physicists would appear to suspect? In the following chapters we shall examine how human consciousness interacts with the physical world, as well as evidence supporting other levels of consciousness, such as that of plants and cells. But before we can evaluate such evidence, we need to get a firmer grip on how consciousness, as we perceive it, operates.

THE PROPERTIES OF CONSCIOUSNESS

Our species is known as *homo sapiens sapiens*, which roughly means: *man which is aware of being aware*. According to this definition, our ancestors, as well as our contemporary primate cousins and other more distant mammal relatives along with the rest of the animal kingdom, were and are aware, yet lack the insight of being aware. Perhaps they are incapable of questioning the meaning of this awareness, or perhaps they merely do not recognise awareness any more than the average human questions being aware of our own awareness. Or perhaps they do, but we do not realise it.

Whatever the case, humans are aware of being aware, which is in part the origin of our troubles as well as the key to all of our potential growth. This awareness, however, is completely dependent on input. Without something to make sense of, there would, per definition, be nothing to make sense of. Thus, human senses are a necessity for human consciousness. By human senses I refer not only the basic five senses, but also to the sense of balance and all the other less well-known sensory systems our biological organism provides, along with any paranormal or non-local senses we might possess.

Senses and Self

We rarely award our senses with their proper credit. After all, they will inevitably shape both our view of the world and our view of our selves. Human beings have a strong orientation towards vision as their primary source of information. Our hearing and our sense of smell do not accumulate nearly as much information as our sight. Though speech is our most obvious way of communicating our more complicated messages, we spend much of our time observing subtle cues in those we talk with, especially if they are new acquaintances. Posture, movement, the use of eyes and hands, their positioning in relation to us, and hundreds of other clues add information to what is being said. In fact, much of the time it is not *what* is being said as much as *how* it is being said, that convinces us of a person's objectives or sincerity or competence or whatever else that person is attempting to convey, or that we are attempting to deduce. Of course, the closer in proximity two people are, the more tactile cues may appear, and the tone of a voice can also convey more than the actual words. The more advanced our communication becomes, the more varied our sensory demonstrations and interpretations will become. Between old and close friends, discussions will probably focus on what is actually being said, but in most other cases communication rarely serves the sole purpose of conveying an idea, and our eyes will do much of the interpretation. Take any situation of courtship—between two people in a bar or between a political candidate and the voting public—or any situation of conflict—between two boxers before a fight or a couple in an agitated discussion—and the physical cues are obvious. In humanity's earlier days, before speech and language evolved to the level it is sometimes conducted at today, this form of communication was probably as apparent as it is today in the animal kingdom.

This does not mean that blind people are reduced to a fraction of the input of those with full ocular capacity, merely that blind people perceive the world differently from the sighted. For a blind person, the visual aspects of life are not likely to take on much of a priority, probably shaping consciousness in a slightly different way from one used to relate to the world through sight. One might well ask, for instance, if an issue such as racism would have evolved if we were unable to get hung up on pigmentation. On the other hand, we might have developed an aversion to dry skin or some other feature that separates some people from others without saying anything of the inner qualities of a person. The point is, of course, moot, as long as the overwhelming majority of humans perceive the world visually: visual cues are going to take up a dominant portion of our consciousness. This need not be a problem in itself, but as we humans are often prone to creating value-systems based on differences rather than similarities in order to make "sense" of the world, we often create "ideas" that have no actual counterpart in nature or reality. As Kant pointed out, we have no knowledge of the world as it truly is: we can at best have knowledge of our own perceptions or of the world as we "know" it.

Taking this line of reasoning to a different species, the shift in perception of the world becomes even more apparent. Dolphins, for instance, have excellent vision but also the use of sonar to "feel" the shape of objects at a distance. I imagine that if we humans also could feel the three dimensional shape of each other, rather than using our ocular capacity to view others in a two-dimensional way, we might be more interested in each other's content and less prone to ignore each other due to visually perceived form.

The point of this perhaps slightly diffuse line of reasoning is that the way we perceive the world will invariably have an effect on our consciousness. The importance of this point will become apparent in later chapters, as the implications of consciousness become more fundamental to nature itself than has been previously supposed in materialist circles.

Storing, Making and Using Sense

Input alone does not constitute consciousness; we also need a system to sort and store this input in the form of memory. Memory comes in two basic forms, long-term and short-term. Long-term memory enables us to remember things that happened or were recorded a long time ago; short-term memory allows us to keep in mind what happened a few seconds ago. Without the possibility of storing and retrieving sensory information, consciousness would be all but impossible.

For consciousness to develop, a process such as the one we call "learning" must take place. Exactly what the learning process is no one can say, but it clearly has to do with assimilating information from long- and short-term memory and constructing these in new, meaningful ways. How this construction takes place and what makes information meaningful is also something we really cannot say all that much about. In the name of simplicity, we will tie up the different aspects of information construction together in the term *cognition* or, broader still, *thinking*. Again it should be pointed out that this is not a book about consciousness *per se*, rather it attempts to prove that what we recognise as our individual consciousness survives what we recognise as our individual deaths. Survives, in fact, not only long enough to realise that we have died, but beyond even the point of no return.

The development of consciousness also requires options: the ability to define and express self through a variety of different actions. Humans appear to have options like no other animals on Earth. We can use our hands to create everything from the childishly simple to the unbelievably complex, allowing us to store information outside of our own brains, painted on cave walls, printed in books and burned into computer discs.

Perhaps our sonar-wielding cetacean relatives, the dolphins, have the same or even greater mental potential than humans, but the aspects of their physical surroundings do not require that they develop that potential as humans have, for better or worse. Or, perhaps, they have developed their potential far beyond ours, but in ways we have not yet understood. In any case, it is the ability to control events that gives rise to a sense of self, which we presume in one way or another to be the seat from which consciousness operates; or at least the seat from which we analyse the input we experience and the thoughts we think.

So consciousness needs some kind of input (at least to begin with), a system for the storage and retrieval of said input, and a cognitive process to make sense of it all. To develop its own potential, the options and the incentives to do so are also required. The basic indication of consciousness would thus be the display of independent thought, or the use of memory in combination with independent thought. As we look into consciousness at the cellular level in Chapter 4 the meaning of this will also become more apparent.

A further aspect of consciousness is communication, though this can be a very tricky indication of consciousness. No one would deny that one person whistling to catch the attention of another was engaging in a conscious act, whereas a microwave oven ringing a bell when the timer has run its course may be communicating information, but not consciously. Neither was the defeat of Kasparov by the chess-playing computer Deep Blue on May 11, 1997, a conscious act on behalf of the computer, at least not to the best of our knowledge. Computers operate after a given set of laws and have no real freedom of choice in the sense that humans do, or at least as we presume we have. Neither is there any reason to believe that computers experience a sense of awareness, though perhaps the development of artificial intelligence will eventually result in a conscious machine. As noted before, this is the point from which the two contradicting views originate and diverge. One says that the concept of self along with the supposed free will is actually an illusion, the other that self and free will are at least as real as the material world.

As we are arguing for the second point in this book, there are several obstacles we will need to clear along our path, but before getting on with our search there is one fairly recent and highly significant discovery about human consciousness worth mentioning. It would seem that whatever the nature of consciousness may be, it is perpetually removed from that which it deals with by half a second. Awareness, it would seem, is history.

THE SPLIT SECOND LAPSE

It is commonly supposed that we experience things as they happen, or that we become consciously aware of sensory input the moment our brain receives this information. We become aware of a dog barking only milliseconds after the sound reaches our ears, or we see a tennis ball more or less simultaneously as it is tossed in our direction, allowing us ample time to make the conscious decision to reach out and catch it or not. Consciousness, whatever it is, must after all be instantaneous. How could it be otherwise?

Well, as it turns out, it is otherwise. In 1979 neuroscientist Benjamin Libet published a paper on "subjective referral" implying that practically all of our sensations *and* actions are actually unconscious, taking place before we are consciously aware of them.[4] The cognitive process of awareness, or our experience of our experiencing if you will, actually takes place half a second *after* the experience it is referring to. The object that we reach out to catch is actually caught half a second before we become consciously aware of reaching out and catching it. Somehow, conscious awareness is referred back roughly half a second, so that we experience that thoughts, actions and sensory input take place when they do.

In other words, you are only consciously aware of these words some half second after your brain has registered them. At the point in time that you perceive yourself to be reading this word, you—or at the very least your brain—is several words ahead. Consciousness only appears to be instantaneous because the point of referral is moved back in time. Take a few moments and let that sink in properly.

This phenomenon is known as *temporal referral* and can be compared to the more familiar *spatial referral*. Spatial referral is the reason we experience things in the outside world (Descartes' *res extensa*, if you will) even though everything takes place in the inside world (*res cogitans*). If we hear a plane, or a bird, or someone calling our name, we will experience this sound as coming from outside, even though the event, for all our knowledge, is taking place in our head. It is important to try to be as clear about space and time as possible from the beginning because, as we shall see, much of what we take for granted where these two fundamentals of our universe are involved, simply is not true. Or, perhaps, we had better regard our familiar version of space-time as *a* truth rather than *the* truth. Whatever the case, in the following chapters consciousness will be shown to be something quite different from what we have grown accustomed to.

The implications of Libet's findings are intriguing. On the one hand it is possible to argue that they confirm the materialist view, that human beings are mere unconscious machines nurturing the illusion of conscious awareness. If none of our actions are conscious, why believe in consciousness at all? On the other hand, if none of our actions are conscious then why should we even create the rather unnecessary and complicated illusion of conscious awareness at all? Perhaps we are indeed directed by a "higher self," the actions of which are interpreted by the brain in this way. Or perhaps we have simply misunderstood the process of time and how it relates to mind.

Though theory makes interesting discourse, it is only fact that can ultimately prove or disprove spirit. Having briefly familiarised ourselves with some important aspects of consciousness, it is time to press on towards our sealing of the *Cartesian Cut*[5] by examining the link between the world of mind with the world of matter.

Summary

The true nature of consciousness remains an enigma and, as often as not, the more we learn the less it appears that we have understood. The properties of consciousness include a sensory system which allows us to make "sense" of the world, and a storage and retrieval system so that we can use this "sense" to construct new "sense" of our own. To create a "sense of self" we also need the physical options or possibility to do so, by communicating and ultimately controlling our actions and our surroundings to some degree. The mental process involved in doing all these things we refer to as cognition or thinking and sometimes as free will, though no one can say for sure if this process is pre-programmed or self-programmed. The former implies that it is merely a physical process similar to any other physical process in the world bound by cause and effect; the latter implies that "we" are autonomous beings able to shape our own lives and destinies, beings of matter yet ruled by spirit.

Is the brain all there is to consciousness, or is it merely a "translator"—a machine that links our eternal spirit with our temporal perception of the material world. Is spirit to the brain what the driver is to the vehicle, or is the driver merely a robot, beautifully programmed by nature, no more than an advanced vehicle itself? This is what we wish to find out, and the path towards such knowledge is not as abstract or as mystical or indeed as impossible as one might think.

In the wake of Descartes and Newton, it is clear where we must begin our search: we must find a link between the spiritual and the physical, between mind and matter. If there is reliable evidence that the "non-physical" force of consciousness, or spirit, can indeed influence the physical world, the soul becomes a scientific possibility. This does not instantly make our soul a probability, but it would be a promising first step along the way. And as the saying goes, every journey however long must be dealt with one step at a time.

So can consciousness influence matter? This is the topic of the next chapter.

III

MIND OVER MATTER

*D*oes *mental intention directly affect the physical world, without an intermediary?*[1] This question, posed by Dean Radin, director of the Consciousness Research Laboratory at the University of Nevada, is a crucial one if we are to argue the case of the soul. If the answer to this question is negative, the concept of spirit will pretty much remain a matter of philosophical discourse and religious faith. If the answer is positive, then the concept of spirit must be taken seriously, and may even be acknowledged as a possible creative force by mainstream science in the not too distant future and studied as such.

Fortunately for us, the answer to Radin's question turns out to be *yes*. The statistical and experimental evidence is quite overwhelming. So overwhelming in fact that few previously decidedly sceptical scientists retain their opinion after reviewing the available data. Let us therefore review some of the more recent research into mind over matter, or psychokinesis as it is also called, along with the arguments for and against the results.

INFLUENCING OUTCOME

One of the largest studies to date is the Princeton Engineering Anomalies Research (PEAR) programme,[2] established in 1979. The idea of undertaking research at PEAR into how mind may affect matter, or more specifically, how conscious intent may affect sensitive electronic circuitry, originated from results achieved at Boeing Research Laboratories. This data implied that people and machines interacted on a quantum level in some inexplicable way.

Robert G. Jahn, Professor of Aerospace Sciences and Dean Emeritus of the School of Engineering and Applied Science at Princeton University, was approached by a graduate student who wished to develop an electronic device which could measure these effects. Jahn, sceptical of the reported effects but open to the potential pedagogic benefit of the project, agreed to review the literature before committing himself to the project. Two years later Jahn was still sceptical, but felt a growing concern with the implications of the first experiments. The man/machine anomalies suggested that crucial electronic systems might be vulnerable in ways previously unknown. A thorough study into the matter was in order, which resulted in the PEAR programme. What one set out to observe were "*...interactions of human consciousness with various physical devices, systems, or processes resulting in statistical output characteristics significantly deviant from those expected on known scientific mechanisms.*"[3]

More simply put, the researchers were to study if, and to what extent, mind influences matter or material devices. Supervising this research apart from Jahn were psychologists Brenda Dunne and Roger Nelson.

To determine if humans could influence the outcome of physical processes without physical interaction, the team used a Random Number Generator (RNG), a system originally pioneered by physicist Helmut Schmidt at Boeing Industries mentioned above.

The main reason that a random numbers generator was selected as the physical system to be influenced was the assumption that such a device should be easier to influence. This device produces zeroes and ones in a random pattern, and is equally prone to produce either. Mentally nudging it in one direction or the other should therefore not demand any great mental effort, as this does not demand that the physical system behave in any "impossible" way.

METHOD AND RESULTS

During each individual trial, the designated test-person or subject is instructed to mentally influence the outcome of the random number generator, to "will" it to behave in a particular way. The subject is not allowed to come into physical contact with the RNG or influence it in any known way, but is told merely to concentrate

on it in order to influence it with mind alone. The possible outcome of the subject's intent will then either result in the RNG displaying numbers around average, significantly above average, or
significantly below average. If the result is either of the latter two,
the implication will be that human consciousness does indeed
influence physical devices. For these purposes, it does not matter
if the subject was, for example, aiming for an above average result
yet achieved a below average result, the result will still indicate
that intent or consciousness influenced the outcome (as it deviated
from average). Thousands of such trial tests were done over a
span of several years at PEAR's laboratories involving many different subjects. Did it turn out that mind could influence matter?

Yes, it did, and though the results were only slight, they were
nevertheless statistically significant. This means that, by common
scientific standards, the results cannot be explained by pure
chance, or at least that they would not be explained as chance
under any other scientific circumstances. And if the results cannot
be explained as chance, the only explanation left is that consciousness is the culprit. Mind influences matter. The gentle nudging of
electrons may seem like a small step for mind, but it is a giant leap
for mind-kind. Far more significant than walking on the moon, it
implies a fundamentally different relationship between the mind
of man and the world man populates than previously embraced
by science.

If the PEAR laboratory was the only one to demonstrate the
phenomena, one might perhaps argue that some unknown factor
in this particular laboratory was responsible for the effect rather
than consciousness, but this was not the case. Examining all the
RNG experiments between 1959 to 1987, some 832 studies done by
68 different investigators, Radin and Nelson jointly concluded that
overall results produced odds against chance by a trillion to one.
That is to be compared with the corresponding control results,
when RNGs were not influenced by anyone consciously, of well
within the chance levels of two to one.[4]

The overall effect of conscious intent was, as noted, slight—
calculated to be 51 percent, where pure randomness would correspond to 50 percent—but this is beside the point. Mind affects
matter, and an effect is still an effect, however slight. That there
was any effect at all should be enough to shake the very found-

ations of scientific materialism, or scientism as this school of thought/faith is also called.

The body of scientific evidence for mind over matter goes well beyond this, however, as random number generators are only one of the many "representatives" of the physical world that have been shown to be under the influence of consciousness. Even the grandfathers of random number generators, dice, seem to fall prey to human intent.

LOADING THE DICE

Research into influencing the results of cast dice began early this century, by J.B. Rhine, Louisa Rhine and their colleagues at Duke University. Trials with dice have since been replicated, criticised and modified several times, and some fifty-two investigators have published the results of 148 such studies in the English language alone.[5] The procedure is quite simple: a die face is specified and when the die (or group of dice) is tossed, the subject wills that face or number to turn up. Each time the intended face turns up, a hit is scored. If the number of hits is more than would be expected by chance, this is assumed to be evidence of mind-matter interaction. Naturally, several arguments can and have been made against the obvious flaws in the experiment. The dice may not be perfectly shaped and the different indentations may influence the dice to fall in less than random ways, or the person tossing the dice may in some way manipulate the outcome. Still, taking all these factors into account, and analysing the full body of data available in 1989, Dean Radin and psychologist Diane Ferrari came to the conclusion that the statistical odds against chance in this study remained over a billion to one. Again it would seem that human consciousness influences the physical world. Again, this influence is slight, but the effect is scientifically reproducible and statistically sound which makes it, in the strict parameters of science, real. Neither do we require a huge influence for our purpose; we need only show that the mind, that consciousness through intent, has enough power to influence the electrochemical switches of the brain in a significant way.

INFLUENCING THE LIVING

Though it is obviously significant that consciousness affects the physical world, it would thus be even more interesting to examine the extent to which consciousness can influence a living organism—especially the brain and nervous-system of the living organism. So are living organisms perhaps more sensitive to this kind of influence than are RNGs or dice? As the influencing force is consciousness, this would not seem to be an unreasonable prediction to make. If spirit or consciousness is the prime influence behind our own personal organism, why should it not be able to influence other organisms also? We will be looking at the interaction of consciousness and other living systems throughout this book, but one specific experiment stands out as particularly important at this point and deserves comment.

PEEK-A-BOO

One commonly experienced sensation is that of being stared at without actually observing anyone doing the staring. Maybe it's the hairs on the back of the neck that start to tingle, maybe it is a tickle at the base of the skull or just a strange sensation of being observed, but almost everybody seems to have experienced this particular sensation at one time or another. Even the feeling of "being thought of" is sometimes connected with physical phenomena. For instance, warm or reddening ears are jokingly attributed to the notion that someone is thinking of the proprietor of the ears in question. So, is there any truth to this uncanny sensation and what folklore attaches to it?

When this sensation is studied in the modern laboratory environment, the person observing and the person being observed are separated and placed in two different rooms. Various devices are then connected to the subject about to be observed (who is commonly referred to as the receiver), which monitor the behaviour of the autonomous nervous system. The observer (also known as the sender), is then instructed to look at and focus on the receiver over a closed-circuit video system during specific but random periods of time during the course of the experiment. Between these intervals, the sender is instructed not to look at or in any other specific way concentrate on the receiver. The latter has no way of knowing when he or she is actually being focussed on, and is usually not even consciously aware of any reactions taking place in his or her nervous system, which is why monitoring is necessary.

Though this phenomenon has been studied and the test procedure modified and improved in several different ways over the years, the size of the effects remain both constant and some of the highest reported. Size, in this case, means how often the subject's autonomous nervous system reacts to the subject's being stared at. If chance expectation is represented by the value of 50 percent, the overall effect of all the studies is an impressive 63 percent. Compared to random number generators, this would have corresponded to a series of numbers that, on average, deviated largely rather than slightly from what would be expected by chance. As Dean Radin points out, this is *"remarkably robust for a phenomenon that—according to conventional scientific models—is not supposed to exist."*[6]

There remains some controversy here, not concerning the reliability of the evidence itself, but as to what it is actually evidence of. Though at first glance it seems a clear-cut matter of psychokinesis—of one person's mind affecting the matter of another's body—what we might actually have evidence of here is *telepathy*. It is possible that the mind of the observer is unconsciously in contact with the mind of the subject, who in turn subconsciously causes the physiological reactions in his or her own body. As will become evident when we review further experiments, it is often impossible to say with any certainty which specific "parapsychological" phenomenon is being uncovered. Fortunately, as will also become evident, this is of no major significance as any expression of consciousness moving outside its traditional scientific boundaries supports the independent state of consciousness and helps prove the case in favour of the soul. Neither is the experiment above the only example of the mind's ability to influence bodies at a distance.

Getting On Peoples' Nerves

Psychologist William Braud has reported the largest systematic body of experiments which influence humans solely through the effect of consciousness or mind. The many experiments contributing to this body of evidence were mainly conducted at the Mind

Science Foundation in San Antonio, and consisted of participants attempting to influence the nervous systems of receivers, both human and animal. Senders and receivers were always separated from each other by distance, sometimes several miles, and sometimes by special soundproofed and electromagnetically shielded rooms. The senders would then attempt to mentally influence the receivers in various ways.

Measuring several different physiological effects such as blood pressure, heart rate and muscle tremor, the 37 different experiments comprising 655 sessions, 153 senders and 449 receivers produced results in odds against chance of more than a hundred trillion to one.[7] In other words, the likelihood that the effects measured in the nervous systems of the receivers were simply due to chance corresponds to the likelihood that if you flip a coin it would land on the same side more than 46 times in a row. If you do not find this very impressive, imagine instead a roulette table that consists not of the numbers 1 through 36 but 1 through 100,000,000,000,000. Such a table would, if it were square, have sides some 300 kilometres long, and if you wanted to place a bet somewhere in the middle, you would have to walk several days to get to the 3 by 3 centimetre square that has your lucky number inscribed. Of course, when the giant wheel finally stopped rolling, if the little white ball did not end up on your number your bet would go to "the house" which here represents the reality of psychokinesis or some other phenomenon that is not supposed to exist according to the materialist view of the world. Unless these experiments were seriously flawed, which no critical investigator has so far managed to demonstrate, we have an almost unbelievable amount of evidence supporting the effect of pure consciousness on other living systems. But perhaps it takes more than this unbelievable amount of evidence if people are to believe something as unbelievable as mind influencing matter.

If this were not enough to seriously reconsider our view of the universe and the role of consciousness therein, there exist at least a further 130 publications dealing with similar experiments of consciousness influencing living systems. The living systems in these cases have not only been humans but everything from cell cultures, plants, mice, hamsters and dogs. Of these studies, 56 reported results with odds against chance of a hundred to one or better. These experiments taken together result in odds against chance of more than a trillion to one, making another robust case for mind over matter.[8] Nor does human consciousness appear to be anything special as experiments with animals have demonstrated that the psychokinetic ability of consciousness is quite neutral to species.[9]

POSSIBLE EXPERIMENTAL FLAWS

The above-mentioned statistics may sound impressive but, as any sceptic worthy of the name will tell you, numbers mean nothing if the experiments they refer to do not meet scientific standards. Indeed, more often than not, experimental results that deviate greatly from the expected are due to flaws in the experiment.

Though it is not the purpose of this book to go into a lengthy discussion concerning the scientific credibility of the experiments related here, a few arguments against them need to be addressed.

Naturally, the perfect, flawless experiment does not exist, be it in physics, medicine, psychology or parapsychology. There is and will always be room for improvement, as indeed has been the case with the different experiments presented here. The routines and set-ups are constantly being improved for each new generation that takes them on, often thanks to sceptics pointing out possible flaws. If the effects measured at these tests were due to basic flaws in the set-ups of the various experiments, one would assume that the effects would become less over time. In other words, one might expect that the better the experiments became, the less impressive the outcome, until finally the perfect, flawless experiment is developed and the outcome would be nil, no evidence of mind over matter at all. Contrary to this, the outcome of the experiments has not changed significantly, despite the fact that experiments have indeed become less possibly flawed over time. This in itself implies that the effects are real.

A second argument is that the effects are not particularly impressive compared to the tricks that professional magicians and illusionists are capable of. This is undeniably true. If a magician or illusionist can make an elephant disappear into thin air on a stage surrounded by hundreds of people, how hard can it be to slightly "nudge" a random number generator in one direction or another. Obviously no one would be particularly impressed if a magician's act was to set up such an apparatus on stage and have it spit out numbers slightly higher than average. Rigging such a machine would be no more difficult than the simplest of card tricks, though the entertainment value would be infinitely less. Another contradiction that magicians often comment on is that the "smarter" an audience is, the easier they are to fool. Education, it seems (to incorporate the saying accredited to P.T. Barnum), breeds suckers. Highly educated scientists should therefore, if this observation is true, be extremely susceptible to fraud.

Well, it turns out that highly trained scientists are not such suckers after all. To avoid being fooled, many researchers nowadays collaborate with magicians when they design experiments to minimise the possibility of fraud. Combining this with the fact that the often randomly selected participants are rarely if ever highly skilled illusionists but "ordinary" people, we are left with a fairly strong case against both flaws and cheating in general.

Furthermore, the people behind these experiments and studies are almost always highly respected scientists who would not openly present results so controversial to contemporary thinking unless they were absolutely certain that the results were indeed valid. To do otherwise would be to invite the ridicule of their peers as well as risk their own standing in the scientific community. Finally, the interpretation of the data is done by experienced statisticians to avoid any misinterpretation. On the whole, the popular argument that pseudoscientific mavericks conduct these experiments is quite false, and those who require further corroboration have only to follow up on the footnotes provided at the end of the book. Scepticism, combined with an open mind is, as always, the best policy.

The question that seems to spring to the sceptical mind at this point is usually: *if this is true, why haven't I heard about it before?* A good question, but one that at least partially answers itself. These findings are indeed quite incredible and demand that we completely reappraise our view of the physical universe, which would demand not only that we must discard much of what we believed in before, but also embrace completely new ideas that are frighteningly close to the mystical. The general view of the scientific community and the scientifically interested public is that parapsychology belongs in the tabloid newspapers, right up there with the extraterrestrial clone-baby bearing a fleeting resemblance to Elvis. Most self-respecting newspapers and televised news shows that enjoy the respect of the public are understandably not all that inclined to report these "kooky" stories for fear of being compared to the tabloids. Of course, the fact that the scientific establishment under the ruling paradigm is even less inclined to publicise and accredit such reports does not help the matter much either, so that *one not having heard about this before* is a state only to be expected. Fortunately we seem to be approaching an era where more and more books, newspapers, magazines and television shows are taking the phenomena seriously, which also seems to hold true for people in general. The very fact that more people are taking a serious interest in the phenomena might prove beneficial to the shift in paradigm at another level, as we shall see from the next example.

When Two Heads Are Better Than One

As has been demonstrated in numerous experiments, if an individual focuses his or her attention on a physical object or system, that system is affected in various ways. Dice have a tendency to fall in a less than random way, electronic circuits behave in more orderly ways than they are supposed to and the human nervous system responds to a significant degree, whether the human is consciously aware of this reaction or not. In short, the focused attention of a single source of consciousness, a single mind, influences the world in subtle ways. It would seem logical, then, to assume that the joint effort of several minds should enhance these subtle effects. If consciousness is a force that has the capability to influence the physical world, a greater amount of consciousness might be expected to result in a greater influence. This particular phenomenon is referred to as "field-consciousness" and has been studied by Dr. Roger Nelson at Princeton University, by Professor Dick Bierman at the University of Amsterdam, and the previously mentioned Dr. Dean Radin, all of whom have reached similar results.

Physical fields were first observed, or rather first inferred, in the seventeenth century. Faced with such phenomena as gravity and magnetism, where bodies influence each other without direct contact, the idea of unseen fields was born. As noted, the scientific community did not greet these ideas with open arms, the notion of "invisible powers affecting objects at a distance" sounding too close to magic or religion. Astrology and spiritualism both depend heavily on the idea of invisible forces affecting the life of human beings, and neither are in the habit of adopting methods that endear them to scientists.

Sir Isaac Newton introduced the idea of "gravitons," invisible particles that were exchanged by the heavenly bodies, in an effort to reconcile the notion of gravity with the need for physical contact. Thus it became the mutual exchange of particles that attracted bodies towards each other, not invisible forces. The classical notion of the field was eventually abandoned with the development of quantum mechanics during the first half of the twentieth century. Quantum fields do not exist in the physical way that classical fields were supposed to, neither does quantum behaviour operate within the usual boundaries of space-time. This means that quantum fields are in a sense non-local, that the field is not located in any given region of space and time. In effect, what happens in one region may instantaneously influence what happens in another region, without any energy being exchanged between the two.

PROPERTIES OF QUANTUM FIELD CONSCIOUSNESS

The nature of quantum fields suggest an entirely different reality for consciousness to arise out of than does classical physics. The latter confines consciousness strictly to the locality of the brain from which it can only influence the world in a direct, physical sense, i.e., through the actions of the body. No matter how much the brain thinks, wants or wishes, the world will not be stirred unless the body is compelled to take some form of action. The non-locality of quantum fields indicates not only that the mind may influence matter by thinking, wanting and wishing, but also that minds may influence each other. As expressed by Dr. Dean Radin:

> The idea of field consciousness suggests a continuum of non-local intelligence, permeating space and time. This is in contrast with the neuroscience-inspired, Newtonian view of a perceptive tissue locked inside the skull.

Drawing from both eastern and western philosophies of consciousness, Radin suggests the following properties to our consciousness:

- Consciousness extends beyond the individual and has quantum field-like properties, in that it affects the probabilities of events.
- Consciousness creates order into systems in proportion to the "strength" of consciousness present. Therefore, the more consciousness, the more order.
- This strength of consciousness in an individual fluctuates from moment to moment, and is regulated by focus of attention. The greater the focus, the greater the strength. Ordinary awareness has a fairly low focus of attention, whereas peak states, mystical states, and other non-ordinary states have a greater focus of attention.
- Groups of individuals develop "group consciousness," which is strengthened by the group's focusing on a common object or event, and weakened if the group's attention is scattered.
- If the individuals of the group are all attending to different things, then the group consciousness and group mental coherence is practically zero. Such a group will have insignificant effect on the order of a given system. The maximum degree of group coherence is assumed to relate in some way to the size of the group, the strength of their common focus of attention, as well as other psychological, physiological, and environmental factors.
- Physical systems of all kind respond to a consciousness field by becoming more ordered.[10]

If these assumptions survive the test of time, specifically the order-creating aspect of consciousness, it could be argued that consciousness influences the physical world more than the other way around. Taken to its extreme, one could even argue that consciousness predates the physical world, that not only does it create order in the "physical" world but actually creates the physical world itself[11] (as the physical world consists of quantum wave-particles). Though this line of reasoning cannot be proven at this point in time, it is interesting as it implies that consciousness—in other words, our elusive spirit—is the fundamental force of the universe. If this is the case, then physical death is probably quite irrelevant, as it is the physical world rather than consciousness that is the "illusion." We shall, of course, return to this theme later, but we now move on to examine the evidence of field consciousness and its effect on different kinds of physical systems.

MEASURING FIELD-CONSCIOUSNESS

The basic measurable quality of field-consciousness lies in its organising properties, and what better way to test organising properties than by running a random number generator. If the field-consciousness of many minds focussing their individual attention indeed has the effect of ordering physical systems, the generator should produce a more orderly pattern of numbers during such sessions than it would in general. To test this hypothesis one need only run a RNG while many minds are focussed, and then examine the results. If the resulting numbers become gradually more ordered, field-consciousness must be taken seriously.

So where does one find circumstances where many minds are focussing on something in unison? Dean Radin and his team tested several different situations where shared mental focus might be presumed. These ranged from personal growth workshops, where a dozen minds were present, to such mass events as the Superbowl football game in January, 1996 with 200 million minds paying attention, to the O.J. Simpson verdict in October 1995 (an estimated 500 million minds present) and the Opening Ceremonies of the Centennial Olympic Games in July 1996 (with about three billion people watching worldwide.[12] The results all turned out strongly in favour of field-consciousness.

In all the trials, the random number generators "spontaneously" ordered themselves, in some cases with the odds a thousand to one against chance. To test the hypothesis that different forms of matter would be influenced, the team also used other random number generators based on the detection of radioactive background particles. These reacted in a similar way, proving that different physical systems were indeed affected by field consciousness as predicted.

As the above-mentioned occasions spanned some fairly long periods of time, some moments were bound to be more interesting and attention-getting than others. Breaks for commercials, for instance, were not likely to warrant the same level of focus as such moments as when the verdict in the O.J. Simpson trial was announced. To provide more reliable results, several observers noted the periods they experienced as high interest as well as the periods they experienced that were less interesting. "High" and "low" periods were then taken into account, both when the material was gathered and analysed. The results showed that the random number generators tended to produce results with high odds against chance during periods of "high interest," reverting back to low odds against chance during periods of "low interest." All the results were statistically significant. The random number generators were also situated in different locations during the trials, but nevertheless reacted in the above-described way, also indicating as predicted the non-local nature of field-consciousness.

These tests have been replicated by psychologist Roger Nelson at Princeton University, by psychiatrist Richard Blasband in California and by psychologist Dick Bierman at the University of Amsterdam, all demonstrating similar results.

Forecasting the Weather

Apart from influencing the physical systems mentioned above, field-consciousness also seems to affect the weather. Having attended a number of graduation ceremonies, Roger Nelson of Princeton observed that the weather usually seemed to be just a bit "too good" on these occasions. This led him to ask if the thousands of attending parents, students and alumni were in some way consciously or unconsciously influencing the weather. Bad weather would, after all, make the occasion somewhat less enjoyable. Examining the meteorological data for the days before, during and after graduation over a period of thirty years, Nelson concluded that this might well be the case. The results showed that there indeed was less rain on graduation days than on the days before and after, the average result being about twenty to one against chance. Comparing the data with six surrounding towns, he found that no such fluctuation was observed anywhere else. Over the thirty years, 72 percent of the examined days had no rain at all in Princeton, whereas the surrounding towns only had rain-free days 67 percent of the time.[13] Weather—notorious for its unpredictability and statistical deviations—may not be, of course, as impressive here as they are in the more stable behaviour of random number generators, but the phenomena raise some interesting questions, nonetheless.

Is it the sheer unpredictability of the weather that makes it an "easy target" for consciousness? Weather is something that affects us in ways we tend to forget as we observe the worst of its nature from behind double-glazed windows in the comfort of our homes. Still, long periods of dry spells can destroy an entire year's worth of crops, as can long periods of unrelenting rain. Weather at its most violent can cause floods and fires, destroy bridges, communications, power lines, even whole cities. There are even those who claim that violent weather is on the rise, as are other volatile Earth-movements, such as an increase in earthquakes and volcanic eruptions, though I cannot comment on the validity of these statistics. The Hopi, a Native American tribe charged with guarding and disclosing ancient prophecy at the appropriate time, claim this is because we have abandoned the old ways, and perhaps this is not so far from the truth as we would like to imagine. Millions, probably even billions, of frustrated minds worldwide might not only have an effect on the weather but on the Earth itself, even if such facts as pollution, land-erosion, ozone depletion and global warming are the most significant causes of these phenomena. One wonders if many unfocused and agitated minds have a disrupting rather than organising effect on the physical world. After all, we have only just realised that such a thing as field-consciousness exists, and who is to say what the extent of its properties might turn out to be. The Hopi would seem to have a point, whatever the case

IMPLICATIONS OF MIND OVER MATTER

That consciousness can influence matter without any direct contact is a scientific fact, both theoretically and practically. The implications are mind numbing (or perhaps the term "brain numbing" would be more appropriate) and will, given time, change not only our perception of the world, but hopefully the way we interact with the world as well. The word "interact" rather than "affect" seems to be operative here. As we influence the world, it influences us. As we influence the consciousness of others—directly (in the Newtonian sense of cause and effect) or indirectly (through quantum influence, independent of time and space)—they in turn influence us. We would seem to be more part of the whole than we previously imagined, not only sharing our atoms with the rest of the universe, but our very consciousness.

Defining where one ends and another begins is difficult enough in the traditional view. The atoms of our body are constantly being exchanged, so are most of our cells, our genes are being replicated in our children as we are replicating those of our parents. Defining where one ends and another begins when non-local consciousness is added to the equation is almost impossible. Where do "I" end or begin, if my consciousness can stretch way beyond the boundaries of my body, not only to cause effects in the physical world, but create ripples with other minds, perhaps even blending with them independent of the traditional boundaries of space and time. What then is an "I", that individual consciousness that we are attempting to establish?

But this is a line of thought we need not pursue at this point. It is sufficient that we have established that consciousness does indeed influence matter, and thus the door can be opened to scientific acceptance of the soul.

SUMMARY

After sixty years of experiments using tossed dice and their modern progeny, electronic RNGs, researchers have produced persuasive, consistent, replicated evidence that mental intention is associated with the behaviour of these physical systems. [14]

Consciousness affects physical systems. These physical systems are as diverse as random number generators, dice, the weather and the human body. The assumption of Newtonian physics, that the physical world can only be influenced by physical forces, has been proven to be at fault. As it gives way to new observations and new theory, so must the fundamental argument against the soul that it implied. However, that consciousness influences the physical world, even to the extent of creating order, does not prove that humans have a soul, nor does it prove that consciousness survives physical death, but it does make this option a real possibility. The soul can no longer be brushed off as mere religious superstition or as a mental invention to make bearable the knowledge that we must all eventually die.

Consciousness is obviously more than an illusion created by the advanced bio-computer of our brain. Who is to say that consciousness even originates from the brain to start with? Perhaps the brain is a mere relay station for consciousness, or its focal point. This should not be such a strange thought as experiments clearly indicate a non-local nature to consciousness. Consciousness is a force to be reckoned with in its own right, and we have only begun to understand its nature and how it relates to the observable world.

So it can be clearly stated that mind influences matter, that there is some kind of causal relationship between Descartes' *res cogitans* and *res extensa*, between the world of spirit and the world of matter. The next step in exploring this relationship is to examine the connection between life itself and consciousness. If a person has a spirit that survives the death of the body, one we experience as consciousness, this spirit would be expected to be an inseparable aspect of life itself. If it leaves the body at the moment of death and does not cease to be altogether, as most materialists would argue, spirit/consciousness should have some life-sustaining or animating quality of its own. Practically every religious and mystical teaching ascribes such a quality to spirit—something that breathes life into otherwise inanimate matter. That which has spirit is alive, that which lacks spirit is not. In order to explore the possible empirical validation of this connection we shall look into the realm of faith-healing, which has recently drawn the attention of medical science.

IV

FORCE OF LIFE

Healing is what people in the medical profession do. The term "healing" itself, however, has lately become synonymous with various practices that more often than not fall outside the boundaries of mainstream medical procedures. When the concept of "healing" is invoked today, a vast number of practices—from healing crystals and magnets to sound waves, hypnosis, prayer and massage therapy—are bunched together. The forms of healing referred to in this chapter are such methods where the practitioner or healer is not in any direct or indirect physical contact with the patient or life-form being healed. Though I have referred to this previously as faith-healing (as opposed to healing in general), this is not an adequate term as many practitioners of faith-healing are in direct contact with their subjects. For the purpose of this chapter we will only examine such experiments where the healer or healers were not in any direct contact with the focus of their healing energy, and henceforth, as the term healing is used, it will denote only such practices. The most correct term would probably be "non-local healing," but in the interest of readability I will adopt the shorter term for the duration of this book. As we review the experimental data, the difference between this kind of healing and other kinds of healing will become clear.

Healing, both non-local as referred to here as well as most other esoteric practices, has been eyed with suspicion by the modern scientific medical tradition. Naturally, there has always been competition between the "old ways" of shamans and witch doctors and the newer ways of doctors, nurses and hospitals, but the scepticism runs deeper than this. Healing simply lies too close to the domain of magic and miracles to be embraced by science.

After all, how could the good intentions of a healer and the abstract movements of hands possibly remove infections, restore damaged organs or cure other ailments inside the body of another human. From the materialist perspective this kind of healing is simply impossible, a relic from a more superstitious age that survives only because desperate people are sometimes also gullible. The reluctance of skilled medical personnel and researchers to look into healing is understandable, since acknowledging that there might be any sense to healing might lend credibility to such "mumbo-jumbo" and the charlatans who practice it. It is hardly surprising, then, that not much serious research into healing exists to date.

HEALING TODAY

During the last couple of decades the science of medicine has fortunately come to acknowledge a link between mind and health. It is now widely accepted that people and animals subjected to stressful environments are more susceptible to various diseases, and that hypnosis, positive thinking and other mental activities may speed up the healing process and even keep possibly lethal developments at bay. We also know that merely telling somebody that they have a terminal disease can seriously damage their health.

The power of the link between mind and body has been demonstrated by researcher H.J. Eysenck. Perhaps not surprising, his study[1] concluded that people who were socially isolated or had problems expressing their emotions—especially negative ones such as anger, grief or fear—were significantly more likely to get cancer than emotionally expressive people. Interestingly enough, repressed feelings actually proved to be even more dangerous to an individual's health than alcohol or cigarettes. This says something about the power of our consciousness, whatever its nature may prove to be. Taking this information into consideration, it seems that a well-balanced mind may be an even more beneficial goal than a drug-free and well-exercised body. Mind affects body much as body affects mind, or so it would seem.

The link between the mind of one person and the body of another has been clearly established (if not yet commonly recognised) by modern scientific experiment, as demonstrated in the previous chapter. As one person can influence the bodily functions of another at a distance, there is no reason why this should not apply also to "healing" in such forms as pain-relief, immune-system boosting, regeneration and more. The usual problem in the realm of parapsychology is also present here, in that no one actually knows how healing works, or how it is connected to consciousness. Indeed, as pointed out earlier it is not supposed to work, so why study claims of it at all? An added problem is the anecdotal nature of most healing experiences combined with spontaneous remission (i.e., when a person simply gets better for no recognisable medical reason), and the many uncontrollable factors that may have influenced the process and the possibility of an incorrect diagnosis in the first place. A serious study of healing will inevitably have a hard time convincing anyone conducting a reasonably sceptical enquiry, considering all the pitfalls.

An example that demonstrates how complicated the issue is from the scientific perspective is the case of physicist Russell Targ.[2] Targ was diagnosed with metastatic cancer of the liver in the winter of 1992 when spots appeared on his CAT-scan plates. The radiologist told him it was a recurrence of a cancer he'd had eight years before. The only medical "cure" was chemotherapy, which might well prove to be as terminal as the cancer itself. Targ, being a physicist familiar with many features of non-local mind as well as being open to healing as an alternative possibility, researched the field thoroughly and received both advice and treatment from Jane Katra, a healer and doctorate in public health. Katra's method of healing began with the conclusion that there were some spots on a film which did not have to mean anything at all, let alone cancer, and included healing imagery, positive affirmations, developing a healthy self-image, a new diet, getting in touch with friends, and much more. Katra even recommended new clothes, new glasses, a new haircut and new behaviours all in order to invent a healthy future for a different person. In the words of Katra:

> The basic idea was to change the host, physically, mentally, emotionally, and spiritually, so the disease would not recognise him. We reduced or eliminated known sources of stress and depression in his life and replaced them with hopeful, peaceful, and empowering activities and environments.

When the time arrived for chemotherapy to start, Targ was already feeling much better. As the doctors took higher-resolution CAT scans to better understand the nature and extent of the illness, the spots appeared quite differently and much less alarming. The question was raised as to the correctness of the diagnosis and permission to do a biopsy of Targ's liver was asked. Targ decided against this as he was indeed feeling better, preferring to wait for further developments, and has been feeling fine since then.

So what was the cause for this seemingly miraculous recovery? The healing energy supplied from Jane Katra? A contact of some kind between non-local minds? Targ's development of a new, healthier attitude? Spontaneous remission? Some other yet-to-be recognised factor? Or a combination of all these? Perhaps the explanation is as mundane as an incorrect original diagnosis due to faulty equipment or some other mix-up. None of those involved can say for sure.

Obviously, the combination of these factors make any single, reliable conclusion impossible. There are simply too many other possible explanations than the scientifically controversial notion of healing, and even if these were not present one could always argue that spontaneous remission was the case. Mere chance, in other words. What is needed to prove that healing actually works on sick people is, as always in medicine, reasonably reliable statistics gathered from repeated trials. Though medical science may seem very calculated and precise, operating much like mathematical equations with specific answers, new drugs ultimately need to be tested on people for their effects to be known with any degree of reliability. The simple reason for this is that no one can say exactly how a new drug will affect people beforehand. Actually, even old and thoroughly tested drugs affect different people in different ways, the result commonly a trade-off between desired effects and undesired side effects. The development of new techniques and new drugs is naturally not a random affair, but it is far from completely predictable as pharmaceutical history clearly demonstrates. Our scientific knowledge is perpetually in a state of development, and the final verdict as always comes from the empirical realm. If it works, it works.

To make a long story short, in order to find out if a drug or a new method works, one does not test it on just one single individual and draw lengthy conclusions from this. Rather one tests it on a larger and preferably diverse group, and draws a careful and preliminary conclusion on the basis of this. This ought also to be the only scientifically acceptable way to find an indication of the significance of healing. So has anyone attempted such a study?

Praying for Health

In 1988, physician Randolph Byrd at San Francisco General Hospital undertook just such a clinical study. One hundred ninety-two patients from a coronary-care unit were randomly selected and their names, diagnoses and conditions were sent to people of various religious denominations who were instructed to pray for them. A second, demographically similar group was selected as a control, and was not prayed for (or at least not in any form organised by or known to Byrd). The objective was to find out if prayer as a form of non-local healing actually worked—i.e., if the intent of a complete stranger could significantly improve the health of another human, without any direct contact. The primary results from this study were actually quite impressive as the prayed-for patients were five times less likely to require antibiotics and three times less likely to develop pulmonary edema than the control group. Further, fewer patients in the prayed-for group died.[3]

Though this study was conducted professionally, sceptics still found possible flaws, such as no one checking if the people selected to pray actually prayed, a lack of information about which prayer strategies were employed, and the fact that the control group may well have had people praying for them also. These arguments may seem strange, as they all assume that prayer might work rather than the opposite, but they remain valid arguments just the same. When all factors were taken into account, the prayed-for group showed between a 5–7% improvement over the control group. This does not exactly constitute a miraculous improvement, and like most other similar studies remains an interesting but inconclusive testament to the power of healing through mental intent. Hopefully, more such studies will be undertaken in the future which may statistically prove the effect.

It is interesting to speculate whether the results of this study might have proved more impressive if only experienced healers had been used. Though healing may well be a skill everybody can learn, some people seem to be more successful or talented at certain skills than others. Perhaps trained and experienced or in other ways skilled healers might be more successful than mere "lay-healers." Supporting this notion is a 1995 study conducted by Dr. Elisabeth Targ and researcher Fred Fisher with distant healers and AIDS patients that showed encouraging results.[4] In Israel, researchers Zvi Bentwich and Shulamith Kreitler also reported in 1994 that patients who received distant healing recovered faster from hernia operations than other patients did. Their surgical scars healed faster, they had fewer cases of elevated temperature, experienced less pain and more improvement in other attitudinal factors.[5]

One might speculate whether some kind of link between the person praying and the person being prayed for might have helped both the focus and dedication of the former group. As reported in the previous chapter, experiments consisting of one person staring at another through a one-way video system proved to be the most successful demonstrations of psychokinetics. If this could be incorporated into the study of healing in some way, these results might also prove more impressive. This stance would indeed seem to have influenced the follow-up study on distant healing of AIDS patients by Targ and Sisher presented in the December, 1998 issue of the *Western Journal of Medicine*. For the purposes of this study, a group of 40 men with AIDS were recruited. Each subject filled out a questionnaire, had their photo taken, their blood drawn, and was paired up with their "statistical twin" (i.e., the person in the group as a whole that most closely resembled them). A computer then randomly assigned one of each pair to the control group and one to the test group. The photos of the subjects in the test group were then sent to 40 healing practitioners of varied backgrounds who were instructed to devote one hour per day for six consecutive days to healing "their" patient. Each week the patients/healers were rotated so each test group patient received healing from ten different healers during the ten weeks of the study. The healing practitioners did not meet their patients, and the patients did not know if they were part of the test group or part of the control group. When the statistics were compared at the end of the study, it was concluded that the control group spent a total of 68 days in the hospital receiving treatment for 35 AIDS-related illnesses, whereas the test group spent

10 days in the hospital for 13 illnesses. The chance of such an outcome, if it were random, is less than 1 in 20.[6]

Of course, though this study might shed some more light upon the efficiency of healing, it reveals little about how healing actually works. As pointed out earlier, the non-local mind works in mysterious ways. Perhaps the non-local mind of the patient senses the intent of those praying and boosts his or her own bodily functions, a case of one's own mind influencing one's own body as suggested earlier. Perhaps one's own mind is being bypassed and the non-local minds of those praying work directly on one's cells. Perhaps the power of life is always around us and all we need do is tap into it. Unfortunately, with healing as with much of the evidence discussed in this book, the answer to the question of how it works remains elusive, and as long as we do not see how it can possibly work from a scientific perspective, a lot of us will be unable to accept that it works at all. Only irrefutable empirical evidence has sufficient scientific clout to change the way we look at healing, and even this may not be enough to sway the most sceptical minds. So is there any other clinically reliable evidence of healing that can not be explained away by spontaneous remission and other factors as difficult to refute?

HEALING AND TEST TUBES

Dr. William Braud of the Mind Science Foundation, mentioned in Chapter 3, has contributed valuable data that might shed some light on the empirical validity of healing. Apart from showing a link between one person's mind and another's bodily functions (such as galvanic skin response and blood pressure), he also had subjects attempt to influence the performance of red blood cells. These experiments entailed placing red blood cells in test tubes of distilled water, which is a hostile environment if you happen to be a red blood cell. Unlike the plasma normally surrounding the blood cells, distilled water lacks salt, which results in the weakening of the cell's walls and eventually causes its contents to leak out. The medial term for this process, which is quite fatal for the cell, is *hemolysis*. The speed and extent of hemolysis can be measured by shining light through the solution, as the transmission of light increases with the decay of blood cells. In each test, the subject would sit in a separate room from the one with ten test tubes containing red blood cells and ten control test tubes with the same content. The subject would then attempt to keep the blood cells of the designated ten test tubes alive (i.e., intact) for as long as possible through healing intent, while the red blood cells of the ten control tubes had to fend for themselves. Braud found that subjects attempting remote healing managed to significantly retard the hemolysis of the red blood cells in the tubes they were attempting to protect as compared to those left "on their own." Another interesting finding: the subjects who produced the most statistically significant results, i.e., the most successful healers, were slightly better at protecting their own blood cells than those originating from someone else.[7] This is interesting as this indicates a stronger non-local link between our own consciousness and aspects our own body, as compared to the body of another. When we look into the research of Cleve Backster in the next chapter, these results will make more sense, as the non-local link between mind and body deepens.

In another experiment, American healer Olga Worrall, working with physicist Dr. Elizabeth Rauscher and biologist Dr. Beverly Rubick, attempted to heal *E. coli* bacteria that had been poisoned with tetracycline. After four hours of exposure to the antibiotic, all of the control bacteria had died, whereas a significant number of the bacteria to which Mrs. Worrall had been directing her healing efforts remained alive.[8] Interestingly, the healer was not able to increase the growth rate of a healthy bacteria colony, only aid bacteria that were in need of healing.

Nor are these the only studies that lend validity to the phenomenon of healing. Psychiatrist Dr. Daniel Benor reviewed over 150 controlled studies into healing on organisms in 1993. These ranged from studies on enzymes, cell cultures, bacteria and yeast to plants, animals and humans and are discussed in his book, *Healing Research*. More than half of these studies demonstrate significant effects of healers.[9]

HEALING BY PROXY

When treating people through, for instance, medication, it is only natural to presume that the ensuing difference in the patient's health is in some way linked to the treatment. Few people question why pills work, and those who do can be shown impressive charts that demonstrate how different substances chemically interact with the body. The multibillion dollar pharmaceutical industry puts a great deal of time and money into these studies, after all. One wonders if healing or life-promoting "energy" (whatever it is) can work in a similar way? For instance, could drinking water be treated by a healer and then used for healing purposes, and if so, what would this tell us about healing? Indeed, what would this say about the force of life itself, if "non-living" systems can contain and redistribute such energy?

During the fifties and sixties Dr. Bernard Grad at McGill University, Montreal, working together with healer Oscar Estebany, attempted to find out if it was possible to affect non-living systems, such as distilled water, in a way that could later benefit living systems. In one such experiment Dr. Grad grew pots of barley seed that he watered with slightly salty water from special sealed vials. Estebany then "treated" some of these vials before they were used to water the seeds. As it turned out, the seeds that were watered with the psychically treated solution grew significantly faster than the seeds that were watered with "untreated" water.[10]

Later experiments by Dr. Douglas Dean and Stephan Schwartz would seem to confirm that a healer can indeed change some of the physical qualities of water, causing it to absorb infrared light differently. Though it is too early to definitely say that healers can improve the life-sustaining qualities of both living and non-living physical systems, it remains possible that this is the case. This would leave us with two options. First, that non-living systems can be improved upon by healers so as to better support life, much as the life-sustaining qualities of farmland can be improved by manure. Second, that seemingly non-living systems are in fact "living" in some basic though not yet understood way. Perhaps these systems can somehow assimilate the healing intent of the healer on some level, and "spread the word" as it were, when it comes in contact with the "living" organic system. Of course, it is also possible that it is the non-local mind of the healer at work. The non-local mind should have no problem knowing which plants will come into contact with the psychically treated water in the future (through precognition, a phenomenon we will address in Chapter 6). The healing intent could then be directly aimed at the right plants when they get watered in what we, from our "local" perspective, would call the future. This may sound abstract and complicated, but considering how abstract and complicated that thing we call life may well turn out to be, the workings of non-local mind are refreshingly simple. And don't worry if you can't grasp this concept of a non-local mind that operates independently from time and space, as there will be plenty of practical examples in the following chapters.

WHAT IS LIFE?

The evidence for healing compels us to again ask what life really is. Whether we believe in the soul or not, most people would agree that there is a difference between a living person and a dead one. That difference is, simply put, life. In the same way there is also a difference between a living cell and a dead cell, though this difference is harder to spot. Still, to the best of our knowledge, a living body—be it a complete human or a single cell—contains the same amount of matter, and the same amount of energy as does the dead one. So what is the real difference? Why does one move about and display conscious intent when the other lies inanimate and gradually decomposes.

From the classic mechanical perspective it is all quite simple. The heart muscle wears out, a blood vessel in the brain bursts, free-radicals finally destroy enough tissue so that some vital organ fails, uncontrolled cell growth destroys a life-enabling system or one of a thousand other reasons causes the biological machine to break down. Simple mechanical malfunction causes the system to collapse, and with the "death" of the system follows the end of the illusion we call consciousness, or at least so some would claim. One might argue that a machine that breaks down can always be repaired by having some or all of its parts replaced, though this seems not to be an option for human beings. On the other hand, this may only be a temporary setback; who knows how long before our knowledge of genetics will allow us to harvest organs from womb-like tanks. Ultimately, from the materialist perspective, it ought to be possible to decode and download into a new machine (i.e., a new brain and body) memories, emotions, thoughts and whatever else constitutes our personality. Through such a process consciousness, or the illusion of it, might survive and prosper indefinitely, or at least as long as there is matter from which to create the human machine. Some information theorists even claim that we will one day all be recreated, which they feel corresponds to an eternal life of sorts. For my own part, I can't take much comfort in the fact that a carbon copy of myself might one day in the distant future roam the world, as it would simply not be "me." But it does raise the rather interesting and central question of exactly what "me" is.

Still, this purely materialistic view of life cannot explain how a healer can keep cells alive in a hostile environment, nor can it explain many of the other beneficial effects of healing. On the other hand, a concept such as "life-force" does. That the cell converts matter into energy which then fuels the body's different processes is evident from what we know about biology. But perhaps there is also some parallel process going on, fuelling not the body as much as the spirit, the conscious communication taking place within the body and non-locally with the rest of the universe. As body and consciousness both ultimately build upon the quantum level, we have one lowest common denominator, one "place" where they both meet. What we see in microscopic biological and chemical processes may not be "causes" as much as "correlation." To dabble a bit in quantum age mysticism, the apparent healing process on the molecular level may only be the result of a more fundamental energy operating at a level we have not yet come to acknowledge.

So life-force may influence the body much as the body influences this life-force. There seems to be a sufficiently similar connection between consciousness and the physical world (as with mind over matter and matter influencing mind in the previous chapter) that these may well be interchangeable. That is, the elusive and undefinable life-force that enables life as we know it, may well be a form of consciousness or spirit. It would seem that consciousness resides in the physical world for as long as the mechanical body allows. A "healthy" consciousness evidently sustains the body longer than an "unhealthy" one (e.g., poor "mental health" can be more lethal than cigarettes and alcohol, as noted earlier). The non-local consciousness of another person, such as a distant healer, may also influence the body in a positive way but ultimately the body must fail and consciousness must depart. No matter how good you are at mechanical tinkering and making things work, eventually you just have to give up on some things because they are bent beyond repair or rusted beyond salvation. Eventually you have to let go of your body. If the quantum level is indeed conscious, then all energy is conscious. What we have then is not life and death, but rather life in different shapes, merely passing from one form into another—which gives us all the more reason to appreciate life in its different guises, as well as all the less reason to fear death.

In the next chapter we shall take a deeper look into different levels and different forms of life in search of consciousness. Perhaps this will shed more light on the connection between life and consciousness.

Summary

If healing actually works, which so far seems to be the case, then we will have established that mind can influence not only the outcome of fairly simple random processes, but also the highly complex processes of life itself. Consciousness, which enables us to experience life, seems also to sustain that life in a very direct and individual sense. Some might even go as far as to argue that consciousness *is* life in its purest form, though this is not something we can rightfully deduce at this point. On the other hand, it is nothing we can disprove. The only fair conclusion to draw from this chapter is that the mystery thickens, perhaps growing a bit too abstract and complicated for our brains to comprehend.

If life and consciousness are invariably linked, it seems reasonable to assume that all living things ought to have consciousness in one shape or another. This is what we shall attempt to find evidence of in the next chapter.

V

GREEN-GREY MATTER

The scene: a Times Square laboratory, New York.
The date: a February night in 1966.
   Actors: Cleve Backster, teacher and polygraph operator for the CIA, and a dracena cane (a large leafed tropical house plant resembling a miniature palm-tree).
Props: a Wheatstone bridge (a resistance recording device used to measure galvanic skin responses and part of the polygraph).

At this point the attentive reader is probably wondering why a plant is listed as an actor rather than a prop in this particular play. If you are, then you're in for the same kind of surprise that Cleve Backster was—a surprise that was to fundamentally change both his personal beliefs and the direction of his scientific life.

Anyway, at this particular date Backster was working late, as he was prone to do, and at some point he noticed that his plants (the dracena was joined by a rubber plant on the windowsill) could use some water. Backster saturated the roots of both plants under running water, and being inquisitive by nature and an experimenter by habit, decided to find out how long osmosis would take. Osmosis is the process by which the plant draws water into its system, and as it happened, Backster had the instruments at hand to measure this. Being particularly interested in the dracena, long-stemmed as it was, he hooked up one of its leaves to the galvanic skin response section of the polygraph. What should have happened then was a slow upward climb on the readout, representing the arrival of moisture in the leaf. This did not happen. Instead the readout showed a downward trend, and the line was serrated, not straight. This downward trend continued for a minute and then, to Backster's amazement, the plant reacted as if it were a human taking a lie-detector test rather than the process of water entering a leaf. Being a leading expert on polygraph tests himself, and not one likely to misinterpret the readout, he decided to cause the plant some discomfort to see if it reacted. First he dunked the leaf into a cup of coffee, but this did not cause the plant to react, probably because the coffee wasn't hot enough. Going for a more drastic approach, he decided to get a match from the other room and burn the leaf. At the same instant he got this idea, thirteen minutes and fifty-five seconds into the readout, the polygraph registered a sudden and prolonged upward sweep. This, in a human, would be interpreted as a reaction of fear.

Backster was baffled. He hadn't even moved, yet the plant had reacted instantly and violently to the mere thought of being harmed. It was almost as if the plant was reading his mind. He left, returned with the matches, lit one and made a few feeble passes at a neighbouring leaf. At this point the plant was reacting so violently that is was impossible to discern any further change. Opting for a different approach, Backster removed the threat by returning the matches to the drawer of his secretary's desk. The plant immediately calmed down again.

The next morning, Backster told his associate, Robert Henson, what had passed the evening before. Henson decided that he too would burn the plant, and sure enough it reacted instantly again. This was the beginning of some of the most surprising research into consciousness of the twentieth century. Though Backster's work is more exploratory and thus less easy to interpret than much of the other research presented in this book, it is both empirical and relates to consciousness and is therefore included here. It could be argued that his findings are not crucial to the central case of this book, but they carry interesting implications as we shall see, and are most likely an integral part of non-local consciousness.

The Secret Life of Plants

In the following decades, Cleve Backster invested a lot of time and energy into researching the "secret life" of plants. This research soon developed to encompass not only the cells of plants, but also that of animals and humans. The evidence of consciousness found at the cellular level, which will be examined in this chapter, Backster named *Primary Perception*. It might be tempting to use the parapsychological term extra-sensory-perception or perhaps plant-ESP, but as Backster points out: "Plants don't have most of the first five senses to begin with."[1] The term "primary" refers to the instant reaction on the cellular level to significant changes in the environment, no matter how far away the cause of the change is. To sum things up, our cells become aware of changes long before the rest of our organism, or at least before the consciousness we think as our "self," perceives anything.

I'm afraid that the concept of "self" will get increasingly more complicated as this book progresses. As we shall see in this chapter, the distinction between our "selves" and our cells is yet another challenge that a modern scientific paradigm will have to come to terms with. Unfortunately few biologists or zoologists have followed up on Backster's experiments. Perhaps this is due to the difficulties of repeatability, demanding an experimental protocol different from what most biologists are familiar with and thus more comfortable with, but on a more fundamental level it is probably due to the implications of primary perception. A world of living, feeling, communicating, and at least to some extent, conscious plants is rather provocative a picture to fit into the framework of the reductionist belief system. If accepted as a fact, much of modern biology and ecology would have to be re-evaluated, and much of its basic assumptions would have to be discarded.

Difficulties with Experiment Design

One problem with designing experiments that Backster, Henson and their associates had to deal with turned out to be that plants only react to "real threat," i.e., the intent to do harm had to be serious. If the experimenters only pretended that they were going to harm the plant, it would not react at all. The plant seemed to sense when the threat was fake and when it was real.

A more difficult problem to overcome was that plants would not react in the same way twice to the same stimuli. When stimulated once, such as being burned, they would react violently, but when stimulated a second time the reaction would usually be significantly less violent, and eventually the plant would not react at all to the specific stimulation.[2] This, from the traditional scientific point of view, is particularly controversial. Scientific protocol demands that an experiment can be replicated, or else its results are regarded as pure fluke, probably originating from faulty experimental routines. Well, more specifically it is only the scientific disciplines that study unconscious processes that demand this kind of repeatability, so perhaps this particular demand is somewhat unfair. In the behavioural studies of animals, such "adaptation" is taken into account, and as it is the behaviour of plants and cells that is studied in these cases, these are the methods and standards that should be applied. Of course, it is probably easier to convince a zoologist than a biologist that plants demonstrate rudimentary consciousness, even if they do not have brains.

A third problem, also to be reckoned with when dealing with consciousness, was that plants had to be surprised. If the plants were expecting something to happen, their reactions would be as weak as if it were something they were accustomed to.

A fourth problem was that plants formed an affinity with humans, animals, other plants and other organisms. Plants seemed particularly inclined to "tune in" to those humans who took care of them, while paying less attention to those who did not have much bearing on their welfare. When conducting experiments, Backster and his associates had to figure out ways to make sure that plants were actually measuring the "right" changes in their environment, rather than tuning into the reactions of their "favourite" human.

A final problem, and a particularly precarious one at that, is that plants seemed to some extent to react according to the intent and expectations of the observer. In plain English: if the researcher really did not want the plant to react, perhaps due to a deep-felt conviction that this was impossible, and an equally deep inability to accept the implications if it actually did, the plant might not react at all.

Taking these problems into the equation, it is easy to see how traditional science has had some trouble in repeating Backster's experiments, though repetitions have been made. On the other hand, the fact that the "Backster Effect", as the phenomenon is known, is no longer a term of ridicule and that Cleve Backster remains a highly respected researcher and lecturer is, in itself, a reason to treat his research with respect. The success of Backster's research is, at least in part, due to the fact that these problems also offered some interesting possibilities and solutions.

BRINE SHRIMP SOUP

Having concluded fairly early that plants reacted to immediate threat as well as actual physical damage, Backster attempted to find out if plants reacted to threats and damage done to living organisms in their surroundings. To do this he would dump live brine shrimp at random intervals into a pot of boiling water in the vicinity of the monitored plant. The instant the shrimp hit the water, the plant would react. Backster assumed that the death of nearby living organisms alarmed the plant as this was threatening despite the fact that the plant had no previous "relationship" to the shrimp.

After repeating this procedure a few times, the plant stopped reacting. It seemed as if the plants became more interested in tuning into Backster than into dying shrimp. So, were Backster's reactions overriding that of the shrimp? To test this, Backster had an assistant purchase new plants which he did not tend personally, and which were stored in a part of the building that he did not frequent. At the last moment, he would attach them to the polygraph so the plants would not form an affinity with any of the researchers. A time delay switch was used, so that the shrimp would be dumped into boiling water when no one was around. This proved successful once or twice, but by the third try the plant usually "lost interest," perhaps because it "realised" that the death of the shrimp did in no way herald its own immediate demise. In any case, it adapted to the situation fairly quickly.

As pointed out above, if the researchers tended the plants for a time, they would form an affinity with their caretakers, and the polygraph readouts would seem to reflect the conversations of the humans rather than the death of the shrimp. This took Backster and his associates some time to figure out, as simply leaving the room was not sufficient to "shake off" the plants. Backster discovered this affinity towards the human provider or caretaker on one occasion when he accidentally cut his finger which, apart from causing him pain, instantly caused a reaction of emotional distress in the plants. Nor did this affinity towards humans seem to diminish over distance. Only by moving the plants to an unfamiliar surrounding and causing some kind of distraction, would the plants pay any attention to the shrimp, and only once or twice at that. All in all, plants seemed to have a special capacity for developing a bond with humans, which allowed for another interesting line of research.

GOING HOME

To test the bond between plant and human caretaker, one must continually monitor the plant and simultaneously keep some kind of track on the behaviour of the human.

It is sometimes claimed that pets in general, and dogs in particular, can "sense" when their masters are returning home, commonly running to the door to greet them. This they do despite the fact that it can take from a few minutes to hours for said masters to return. So, if true, the pets are not reacting to the sound of footsteps along the path, but to the mental decision of their owner to return, or something similar to that. This claim was tested by biologist Rupert Sheldrake, known for his theory of *morphic resonance*,[3] by comparative videotaping of the behaviour of pets at home and their owners at work, which resulted in some support for the claim.[4] As the same relationship seemed to exist between plants and their keepers, Backster tested this by walking about town until he randomly decided that it was time to return to the laboratory. Writing down the time in his notebook, Backster would then return and check the readouts on the plants. Sure enough, the plants reacted favourably at the instant Backster had decided to return home. Apparently they could sense when this was happening, despite being separated by distance. The distance itself seemed to be of no consequence whatsoever.

In other tests, the conversation between humans would be recorded, and the rise and fall of the emotional content would be clearly reflected in the rise and fall of the plant's agitation. Non-local consciousness seems well and alive in plants also.

SINGLE CELL SENSITIVITY

As noted above, this apparent ability to sense and express emotion was not restricted to organisms as evolved and differentiated as plants, but also to such simple organisms as bacteria. More interestingly, the single white blood cells of humans would demonstrate a particularly strong bond to the person they originated from. Backster found that oral leukocytes (i.e., white blood cells removed from a person's mouth), placed in a test tube, would respond electrochemically to the donor's emotional states, notwithstanding if the donor was out of the room, out of the building or out of state. One of the ways this bond was tested and verified was through split-screen videotaping of experiments with the chart readout superimposed at the bottom of a screen showing the donor's activities.

The implications of this kind of communication are, naturally, controversial. Single cells have no brains and are, at least according to the orthodox view, pre-programmed to behave in a specific way. Exactly how this works has not been answered so far, but it has been quite reasonably assumed that such activity is due to neural activity and chemical triggers. After all, in what other way would the brain and the rest of the body communicate short of magic? Yet, here again we have examples of experiments resulting in empirical data that seem to defy logic. Primary perception suggests a completely different and non-local kind of communication, one between mind/consciousness and organism, rather than brain and body. Much as the consciousness of one person can influence the autonomic nervous system of another, as demonstrated in Chapter 3, it seems that the consciousness of the individual can interact with his or her body without using the direct paths of the brain (electrical or chemical communication). The implications for such branches of science as neurology are, of course, quite staggering. But before we get carried away: Are we really talking about an individual consciousness here, or merely a reflection of human consciousness? A mirror can reflect a convincing image of a person, yet we would not accredit that image any autonomy whatsoever. It does what we do, is capable only of reflecting action, not acting independently. Is it possible that plants and cells merely reflect the emotions of their surroundings, in particular those of their keepers?

BRAINY CELLS?

The obvious question here is to what extent cells are conscious. Do cells react according to their own senses and sensibilities or do they simply react to their environment, albeit non-locally? At first glance it may appear that plants merely reflect the reactions of their environment. True, when physically abused (such as being burned), the plant would seem to display independent thought or reaction—but a plant is a living organism even in a mechanistic universe, so some kind of reaction to physical damage is only to be expected. From the materialistic point of view plants are as "alive" as humans, so plant reactions should not be completely impossible to reconcile with this scientific branch, no pun intended. As Backster points out, primary perception does seem to be linked to survival, a fundamental reaction that can easily be programmed into any computer-simulated environment. Supporting this hypothesis is the fact that the plant reacted negatively when Backster accidentally cut himself, mirroring his pain.

But on closer examination, the theory that cells merely reflect the emotions surrounding them conflicts with the evidence. For instance, when Backster considered burning his dracaena, it reacted violently. If it was reflecting Backster's emotions rather than displaying it's own, there should have been no such reaction at all. Backster, after all, had no reason to be alarmed at the thought of burning a plant. The display of both independent thought and memory, two crucial aspects of consciousness, are evident from many experiments. For instance, in one type of experiment, Backster placed two plants side by side in a room and then randomly selected one student out of six whose job it was to act as aggressor and completely destroy one of the plants. After the deed was thoroughly done the student would leave the room, and Backster would return to hook up the remaining plant. Then one student at a time would enter the room; there was no reaction from the plant until the student who had destroyed the fellow plant entered the room, at which time the plant reacted violently. The violent reaction to this particular student clearly suggests that plants have some kind of memory capacity, if only to remember danger. On other occasions, plants would react in a positive way when Backster's assistant, often the designated "bad guy," accidentally hurt himself, which again shows a capacity for independent thought. Not a very charitable sentiment, perhaps, but who can blame them.

There is one final property of cellular consciousness which Backster discovered: that they sometimes "pass out" or lose consciousness. When presented with a severe enough threat, such as being eaten, they would go into "shock" and cease all activity. Backster hypothesises that the reason for this is much as it is with humans: we sometimes simply "shut down" in order to handle mental and emotional overload, so why should not plants and single cells do the same?

For the vegetarian reading this chapter, this will hopefully be perceived as a mitigating factor. Though plants may have emotions much as humans and animals, at least they don't appear to suffer while being eaten and digested. Perhaps they even enjoy becoming part of us, on some level. Perhaps this is what the concept *beyond death* means for plants.

Levels of Consciousness

The display of independent intelligence in plants and cells implies that there are many levels to consciousness. We seem to have an individual consciousness—the one we think of as our "self"—as well as a "primary consciousness" at a cellular level dealing with immediate survival. Supporting the theory of "primary consciousness" is the fact that plants and cells could not only remember, but react according to memory. Using experience to assess and handle a new situation is a basic property of reason or cognition, as related in Chapter 2. Without it, we could not operate very successfully as humans. That consciousness on a human level is capable of far more complicated mental feats (such as arithmetic, language, and other use of abstract symbols) than primary consciousness is primarily due to the options and complexity of the human brain. As we can react to our environment in so many more varied ways than can plants, we not only *can*, but pretty much inevitably *must* develop a more varied form of intelligence. The trade-off is perhaps that we are not as conscious of our environment as a whole as plants are. Or perhaps we are just not as conscious as we could be if we really paid attention. On the other hand, human intelligence may ultimately not only destroy humanity but even the Earth as we know it, which makes plants a lot smarter in the long run. That we humans think we are so smart may be more closely linked to our particular perceptions of intelligence than any objective measurement of evolved consciousness. Objectively speaking, nature on the whole is pretty smart because it functions with so few disruptions and adapts brilliantly to new challenges. Humans so far have managed to disrupt nature more than any other naturally evolved phenomena known to us (apart from possibly the odd comet or geophysical event), which, as we cannot survive without nature, is almost unbelievably stupid.

It would seem that not only consciousness, but also intelligence, comes in many different versions, relating to each other and to the whole in subtle ways. On the other hand, only humans have a consciousness and intelligence of an order high enough to do stupid, irrational things. As our level of consciousness allows us a vast number of alternatives, some of these alternatives will invariably be foolish in the long run, just as others will prove wise. Perhaps stupidity is merely one of the trade-offs that intelligence or consciousness at the human level must learn to deal with.

Whatever the case may be, Backster's observations, along with their implications for consciousness, spark hundreds of new questions, the most important for our purpose being how the primal consciousness of human cells relate to the "collective" consciousness of the human "self" or "soul." Did I say that the issue of non-local consciousness would become more clear as we progressed? I guess things are going to get a bit more complicated before they become simpler.

In the traditional materialist view of the body, humans are alive and consist of human cells that are all individually alive. As consciousness is a collective illusion originating from the brain, individual cells have little to do with consciousness, other than reporting the odd stimuli via the nervous system. The only cells that influence consciousness are the brain cells, popularly termed "grey matter." Brain cells not only influence consciousness, but also constitute consciousness in this view. This is quite brutally demonstrated when the brain is damaged in one way or another; the loss of brain tissue generally accompanies the loss of mental functions. That neuroscience cannot yet explain such enigmas as the half-second delay between the brain registering stimuli and consciousness registering the same stimuli, in no way changes the opinion that the brain is a mere machine operating a complicated programme, but a programme nonetheless.

The evidence presented here again conflicts with the basic assumptions of neuroscience. One such assumption is that all communication in the organism travels along the pathways created by billions of nerve cells known as the nervous system. Clearly the experiments conducted by Backster and others prove that cells successfully communicate in other ways also. Even individual cells with no neural connections at all manage to communicate information between each other. In the case of plants one should also remember that they have no nerve cells to begin with. Obviously, neuroscience can only explain the mechanistic side of human and animal nature, so when it comes to explaining this particular type of communication, neuroscience can offer little help.

THE SUM TOTAL OF CONSCIOUSNESS

So every cell in our body is conscious. Is the sum of our consciousness as simple, then, as the sum of our cells? If we lose an arm, does our consciousness diminish correspondingly to the amount of cells lost, or does our consciousness increase as we add new cells though body-building or feats of nutritional indulgence? Obviously this would not seem to be the case. The connection between cell-level consciousness and "self-level" consciousness is probably as non-traditional as the nature of consciousness is revealing itself to be. It is probably more true that our cells at their primary level reflect the consciousness of our self. This at least seems to be the case with our leukocytes when they are separated from the rest of our body.

To complicate things further, consciousness at the quantum level could be added to the equation. As evident from Chapter 3 the mind does influence (i.e., communicate with), processes at this level, and several physicists argue that sub-atomic behaviour does demonstrate a form of consciousness.[5] Perhaps quarks have a simple "dichotic" consciousness, the ability to choose between different options, to be compared to the more varied primary perception of cells. Sub-atomic particles create atoms that create molecules that create the different parts of cells that create organs, bones, and everything else that creates the human being with our sense of self and our "individual" consciousness.

As the level of consciousness rises (i.e., the acts that consciousness can perform and the concepts that consciousness is capable of grasping), one is tempted to speculate if there is not a level above the human, or perhaps even several such levels. Levels that we can perhaps sense but not fully grasp, any more than a single cell can understand a simple problem of algebra. A level our human consciousness may be a part of, much as our cells with their primary consciousness are in their turn a part of us. The term "individual consciousness" might even be pointless, a mere illusion caused by the fact that we are restricted to live our lives in individual bodies and see all things from a local, individual point of view. But these are abstract questions to be saved for later speculation. The temptation to digress becomes greater the more aspects of consciousness reveal themselves, so it is important to return to the main theme of this book: can individual consciousness survive physical death?

IMPLICATIONS OF PRIMARY PERCEPTION

The foremost implication of this chapter is that consciousness is more than the mere firing of neurones in the brain. Indeed, a brain does not even appear to be a necessary requirement for the basic functions of consciousness. This does not mean that our human consciousness can exist without our brain, but it is clear that mind can exist without brain, which is another step along the path. The non-local qualities of this mind also retain some interesting implications into the nature of our consciousness. If consciousness can "spread out" through time and space, who is to say that it need originate from a point in time and space (the brain) at all? Perhaps it exists elsewhere to begin with, our brain being merely a "homing device" or a "focal point" from which consciousness can translate the world (the *res extensa*) into something we (the *res cogitans*) as separate selves can experience.

This all borders on mysticism, of course, and it is understandable if the scientifically sensitive reader is squirming uncomfortably at this point, so we shall move on. In the following chapter we shall examine what controlled and repeated parapsychological tests have revealed about the nature of human non-local consciousness. Not that this is likely to lessen any squirming, but at least it is less abstract.

SUMMARY

It is obvious now that some aspects of our consciousness, such as emotional reactions, awareness of surroundings, memory and basic cognition exist at the cellular level. This consciousness exists in plant cells, in animal cells and in human cells. Cells originating from the same body are in constant communication with each other and with the body's consciousness as a whole, and this communication is instanteous, whatever the geographical distance separating the cells. Cells also communicate with surrounding expressions of life (and death), sensing threats and sending warnings, as well as tuning into other organisms they feel a bond with. Cleve Backster has named this phenomenon "primary perception", in part because it seems oriented first and foremost towards the survival of the organism.

A significant conclusion to be drawn from this is that consciousness does not need a brain to express itself. Plants, for instance, have no recognised "emotional centre" capable of expressing sentiment, memory centre to store information, sensory centre to recognise danger at a distance, or any cognitive centre to combine all this into an appropriate reaction. And plants definitely have no way of immediately sensing what is taking place in different buildings, different cities or even different countries. Yet they appear quite successful at all this, notwithstanding.

As we have seen in the previous chapters, consciousness affects physical processes, which is the basic prerequisite for spirit, and is intimately linked to life and being alive. In this chapter we have found further proof that every living organism, from single cells and upward, possesses consciousness of a kind. We have also seen that a brain in itself is no requisite for consciousness. This does not prove that our consciousness will survive beyond our death, of course, but clearly this evidence makes it all the more possible. "Possible" is naturally better than "impossible," but it's not quite the same as "probable" or that ultimate, desirable scientific goal: "factual." To press onward towards this destination, we will now explore the width and depth of consciousness as it is available to us humans.

EXPANDING MINDS

S o far we have reviewed some evidence indicating that consciousness can indeed influence the physical world. We have also seen that consciousness, in a very basic form at least, does not require a brain. Plants and cells demonstrate a considerable amount of sentience through conscious reactions to their surroundings. The body itself would seem to communicate internally through not only the traditional neurological pathways but through non-local consciousness also. In the same sense, bodies/minds seem to influence each other through means other than the traditionally recognised direct or local communication. Consciousness is evidently more than the complex information exchange between neurones within the skull, seeing as it can reach out, communicate and influence the physical world without using the body as an intermediary. Though it is interesting to note that consciousness as such can exist (i.e., perform acts demanding consciousness) without a brain, what we need to find out is if our own individual consciousness, apparently residing in the brain, can exist *without* the brain. In the following chapter we will study dimensions of human consciousness that are just beginning to be probed in the modern laboratory environment. This in order to find out how far outside the brain, in terms of space and time, the mind can exist.

AND YET SHE MOVES

ExtraSensory Perception, or ESP for short, is frowned upon in most scientific circles. Though several scientific dignitaries over the years have speculated that there may be more to it than meets the eye, metaphysically speaking, and though many scientists believe in such a thing as the soul as well as some godlike force, research into the matter on a practical level is discouraged. That one may entertain theoretical ideas seems acceptable, yet there seems to be a strong taboo against attempting to find empirical proof of them.

Though this might strike one as an odd state of affairs at first, in actual fact it seems to be little more than human nature at work. While new theories may be thought-provoking, they rarely threaten the dominant theories within the scientific field. There are exceptions, such as the theory of natural selection or the theory of general relativity, but these are rare. New *findings*, on the other hand, do threaten dominant theories. And nobody enjoys having his or her view of the world threatened. Even more fundamentally, attempting to find evidence of ESP is considered a futile endeavour, a waste of time and money, as within the dominant system of thought such phenomena simply cannot exist. There is no room for magic in a universe of mechanistic law, of cause and effect, as the materialist would argue.

The astronomer Galileo is rumoured to have whispered *eppur si moeve* ("and yet she moves") under his breath when he was forced to renounce the notion that the Earth circled the sun rather than the other way around. Though it is not very likely that these words actually escaped him at the time, the observation they expressed would appear relevant to our situation today. Though the accepted frame of thought in the 17th century was that the Earth lay at the centre of the universe, Galileo's observations clearly showed that this was not the case. He also discovered four moons orbiting Jupiter through his telescope, another observation that could not be reconciled with the dominant view of the celestial spheres dating back to Aristotle. Empirical evidence, however, was no match for the paradigm of the time. The Earth did not orbit the sun because it was common knowledge that the Earth was the centre of the universe. And Jupiter could not have four moons because this would mean that there were a total of eleven heavenly bodies, not the religiously significant seven recognised at the time. These were the grounds that allowed traditionalists of the time to completely ignore the evidence provided, and even to denounce the value of the telescope, since it came up with such ridiculous information. It's an interesting story if for no other reason than it has repeated itself a number of times since then, and is likely to repeat itself in the future. There is a lesson to be learned here: no matter how reliable the evidence one might produce, if it flies in the face of the reigning paradigm, it will never be enough. In the case of parapsychology, the much frowned upon discipline dealing with ESP and other "ridiculous" concepts, the offence is as deep as Galileo's suggestion that the Earth actually circled the sun and that Jupiter had moons. If you feel that ESP is indeed impossible, but feel an uncomfortable twinge at this comparison, then good for you, you might not fall prey to the same mistake. On the other hand, if you think that ESP is impossible because it so obviously flies in the face of fundamental scientific standards and are offended at being compared to those archaic idiots who refused even to review Galileo's empirical evidence because of their pseudo-scientific standards, well that is your prerogative.

Yet despite this obviously hostile climate, researchers (many of these actually engineers or physicists or psychologists and not "merely" that dubious creed parapsychologists) have managed to accumulate an impressive amount of evidence in favour of Extra-Sensory Perception and have begun constructing theories about both the process as such, as well as the implications. The scientific evidence of psychokinesis was explored in Chapter 3 of this book; in this chapter, other aspects of our non-local consciousness will be addressed, as will the implications of the phenomena for the postmortem survival of our consciousness.

Terms of Parapsychology

The bulk of parapsychological research that exists can be divided into three areas that invariably overlap, namely *telepathy*, perception at a distance (also known as *clairvoyance)*, and perception over time (also known as *precognition)*.

Telepathy consists of cases where one mind supposedly communicates information to another whereas clairvoyance (or clear viewing) deals with cases where the mind gathers information without using our ordinary senses. Precognition (or advance knowledge) refers to such cases wherein consciousness gathers information that does not yet "exist" in linear time, information of things yet to come, as it were. There is also a reverse form of precognition known as *postcognition,* which deals in a similar way with that which has passed. With ESP, it is usually impossible to deduce with any reliability which is which. For instance, in a seemingly clear-cut case of telepathy a person might be describing the simultaneous activity of someone else at some distant location. However, this might in actual fact be a case of precognition, as the person in question might be describing his or her own future knowledge of what the other person's actions were at the time. In effect, our subject might be unconsciously experiencing memories of the future rather than memories of the past, so to speak. This may sound farfetched, but as we shall see, not only space but also time seems to have different properties in the strange and fascinating world of parapsychology.

Fortunately for our search, it matters little how the different phenomena are categorised as they all are expressions of non-local consciousness in one way or another. Non-local consciousness has its own value for us, as it is the part of our mind that is not restricted to the here-and-now, but is free to gather information from pretty much any point in time or space. Though this may sound like an episode of *The Twilight Zone,* we shall press on to examine a few specific methods used when researching non-local consciousness. Not that the sense of the twilight zone is likely to diminish, but at least there is some comfort to be found in scientific method—especially in a world gradually appearing more similar to the aforementioned zone.

Ganzfeld Telepathy Experiments

Sensory deprivation, resulting in reduced activity in our ordinary senses, is commonly acknowledged to cause especially receptive mental states, sometimes bordering on the "mystical." For instance, sensory-isolation chambers in which a person is shielded from sound and vision and is floating on saltwater of body temperature can induce highly suggestive mental states. While in this state it is possible to make hypnotic suggestions to the subject (such as *"your craving for nicotine is diminishing,"*) which will have a far greater impact than a similar suggestion spoken in ordinary surroundings to an ordinary state of mind. Similar states can be reached through various methods of meditation, by use of certain drugs, in both the dreaming state and prior to falling asleep (known as the hypnogogic state) and under hypnosis. Though in the case of the sensory-isolation chamber the suggestion is delivered to the ordinary senses, it seems reasonable to assume that the mind should also be exceptionally receptive to extrasensory information in this state. It therefore seems logical that if one is to study telepathy, or any other aspect of non-local consciousness, these are the states of mind that will provide the best results. In the early seventies, three researchers, parapsychologist Charles Honorton, and psychologists William Braud and Adrian Parker, independently came to the same conclusion. Each researcher decided to study the phenomenon of telepathy using a sensory deprivation technique called the *ganzfeld*, which is German for "whole field." The basic idea, according to Dean Radin, *"was that if a person was placed in a condition of sensory deprivation, the nervous system would soon become "starved" for new stimuli, and the likelihood of perceiving faint perceptions that are normally overwhelmed by ordinary sensory input would improve."*[1]

The ganzfeld-telepathy experiments had several advantages over earlier experiments and turned out to be particularly interesting in terms of providing reliable scientific evidence. It proved also to be a very efficient way of studying the phenomena (as earlier efforts demanded more time and effort and were generally more complicated to interpret). Most importantly, perhaps, the method offers specific guidelines as to how experiments should be conducted and evaluated, allowing for that bastion of scientific faith: independent reproduction.

The ganzfeld method has three stages: preparation of receiver and sender, sending of target, and evaluation of outcome, which provides a separation of the sender, the receiver and the conductor of the experiment as well as an unambiguous way to measure the outcome. In a typical session the receiver is positioned in a secluded room in a reclining chair, wearing headphones and some opaque shielding over the eyes (such as table-tennis balls cut in half). The headphones will produce so-called *white noise* (basically static, the kind you find between radio stations or on television channels after transmission has ceased) and a red light will be shone at the receiver's face. Eventually the brain becomes starved for new visual imagery or changing sound; at this point, impressions may pop up in the mind; the receiver is instructed to continuously report these impressions into a nearby microphone. At the

SKAGIT VALLEY FOOD CO-OP

202 South First Street
Mount Vernon, WA 98273
360-336-9777   www.skagitfoodcoop.com

6/09/2013   7:19 PM   615963
2   Christal
85761025585   MINI SIDEWALK CHALK   2.49
72609033130   ALDENS LT VAN ICECRM* 5.99
Patronage Redemption   -8.68
SUBTOTAL   8.48
WA Sales Tax   0.20
TOTAL   8.68
PATRONAGE ELIGIBLE   8.68
TOTAL TENDERED   8.68
CHANGE   0.00

Patronage
Earned: $0.00 Balance: $5.20

Today You Saved $1.26

Acct: 23842
Britt Shellenberger

Save receipt for refunds
w/in 90 days of purchase
THANK YOU

Have you moved?
Did you let us know?
Please assure we have your current address

same time, the sender is in another location, concentrating on the randomly selected target or group of targets. These targets may be single images such as photographs or illustrations, or sometimes, video-clips, including movement and sound. During the ganzfeld experiment, the conductor of the experiment is not aware of which target the sender had selected or been given, and is in fact as unaware (or as unaware as it is possible to be) of what is being telepathically transmitted as the receiver is. This protocol ensures a minimal risk of contamination due to experimenter influence.

In many cases the receiver communicates his or her impressions directly to the experimenter as well as the sender, though this is commonly a one-way communication. This allows the receiver the comfort of knowing that someone is listening, as the sense of isolation might cause distress that is likely to affect the outcome of the experiment. Also, this allows the reported impressions to be recorded and analysed later, as well as giving the sender feedback, which might in turn help the sender to improve the telepathic transmission of the target. The sender is not allowed to communicate with the receiver, however, as this might influence the receiver.

After the transmitting session is over, the receiver is shown a number of possible targets. The receiver is then asked to identify which target or targets he or she feels most closely corresponds to the impressions previously experienced. Usually, four possible targets are presented to the receiver, who ranks these 1 to 4, one being the most likely target. If the one is accredited to the correct target this is considered a "hit," if any other number is, then it is a "miss." On some occasions, a third party does this correlation, presumably to rule out precognition, as discussed earlier. This means that the statistical rate of hits due to pure chance, over a number of experiments, should deviate only marginally from 25 percent. So, how successful were these experiments in proving telepathy (with the added facilitation of sensory deprivation)?

In a meta-analysis from 1985 comparing twenty-five different experiments totalling a 762 sessions, the overall hit-rate was 37 percent. This corresponds to odds against chance of a trillion to one.[2] In 1997 another meta-analysis was undertaken, including all comparable ganzfeld experiments to date, totalling 2549 sessions from a number of different research facilities in both America and Europe. The overall hit-rate was lower, 33.2 percent, but taking the greater number of sessions into account the odds against chance were far greater: a million billion to one (100 000 000 000 000 to 1). In other words, telepathy, the transmission of information from one mind to another, has a substantial scientific validity. An interesting, if not relevant, observation for our purposes, was that receivers of a more creative disposition, such as writers, artists, actors and musicians, proved to be exceptionally talented, reaching hit rates as high as 50 percent or more, as a group. The highest results appear to be attained by classical musicians—the suggested reason for this being an especially balanced mind between both hemispheres. Where the student of classical music must use the left brain to make sense of the highly complicated sheets of music, the right brain must be simultaneously exercised in expressing this music. Some have hypothesised that brains that are exceptionally well balanced between the hemispheres are also exceptionally well equipped to "pick up" and interpret information non-locally.

The fact that we can reach out and "touch minds" in some sense is no proof that consciousness survives beyond death, of course, but it is interesting as it allows that knowledge can be transmitted through the power of mind alone. As our knowledge is undeniably a part of our identity or sense of self (consciousness without knowledge would undoubtedly be a rather limited affair), evidence of telepathy is of some importance. Also, telepathy represents a form of communication between minds, and communication is another important aspect or component of consciousness, as noted in Chapter 2. If minds can communicate knowledge to each other through the power of thought and intent alone, what else might they be capable of?

I Spy With My Mind's Eye

Of all the experiments designed to explore non-local consciousness, the process known as *remote viewing* is probably the most interesting and the most demonstrative of what our mind is actually capable of sensing. Though this process leans partly on telepathy, the bulk of experiments have dealt with clairvoyance and precognition.

Remote viewing may be so successful because it was originally designed and developed, not for scientific purposes, but for more practical, even sinister, ones. Remote viewing was created to gather intelligence, or to use the more common term, to spy. Before the cold war gradually warmed to a more agreeable temperature, it came to the attention of the CIA, among other agencies, that the Soviet Union made extensive use of "psychics" to gather information. As the common practice in those days was "*if they've got one we want one, too,*" the various US government agencies initiated a program at Stanford Research Institute (SRI) aimed at making use of psychic spies. This objective was enabled through enlisting, among others, the renowned psychic Ingo Swan and physicists Harold Puthoff and Russel Targ.

Though the objective of a remote viewing session may vary, the basic method is the same. The "remote viewer" is asked to sketch and/or describe the designated "target." This target may be a distant location (e.g., a person, an object, a photograph or something else of which the viewer has no direct or indirect knowledge by any ordinary means). In most cases, the remote viewer is accompanied by an interviewer who serves as guide or a coach by asking questions about the viewers impression of the target and offering encouragement. In these cases, the interviewer is of course equally without knowledge of the target's actual nature. Basically, the viewer relaxes and describes whatever impressions come to his or her mind. These impressions are later compared to the actual target.

To many people, this sounds quite ludicrous as it offends every traditional scientific sensibility that has been developed during the last couple of hundred years, and would be quite laughable if it did not prove to be so astoundingly effective in so many cases. In fact, the most talented remote viewers have repeatedly come up with descriptions of the targets in question, accurate beyond anything that could be attributed to chance. We shall look into a few such examples later on.

In most cases, however, the descriptions of targets have been more symbolic than photographic in nature. For instance, remote viewers would quite often be successful in describing such aspects as shapes and structures as well as their relative size and locations, but the nature of these structures would seldom be apparent. Textures, temperatures, colours and other clues into the nature of the target, including its purpose or function, would often be provided by the viewer. Sometimes the viewer would even provide drawings that bore striking similarities to the target, but the nature of the target itself would often remain obscure. Exceptions exist, naturally, as we shall see when we look into the results of some of the most talented remote viewers, but gathering information with one's mind alone would appear to be fundamentally different to using one's ordinary senses.

The early studies were undertaken for various government agencies, the results were forwarded for further analysis to whatever agency had requested the remote viewing and had supplied the target. That these sessions were rarely perfectly accurate in their results should not dissuade anyone, as it is quite remarkable that they were accurate to any degree at all. It is truly mind-boggling that a person provided only with coordinates on a piece of paper to a location where that person had never been (as most locations were highly classified), should be able to describe anything significantly relevant about the location at all. To add to the overall strangeness of the phenomenon, these coordinates were sometimes presented in an envelope that was not even opened. Perhaps this does not strike the average government spy as exceptionally strange, but to most scientists any serious correlation under these circumstances is quite impossible. Yet, remote viewers managed to repeatedly describe these locations with such accuracy that the agencies ordering these descriptions suspected actual breaches in security. In other words, the remote viewers were coming up with information they not only should be unable to come up with by ordinary physical means, but were coming up with information that was also highly classified.

An even stranger aspect of remote viewing is the fact that distance in time seemed to present little more hindrance than distance in space. In several sessions the remote viewer was successful in "seeing" both past and future events which were later verified. In some cases this verification even had to wait several months (one such case is reported below). These cases of precognition are all but impossible to explain in terms of chance, presenting some serious practical and philosophical problems to deal with. Though causality is still a force to be reckoned with, prior knowledge of the future will invariably have an effect on the future, allowing cause and effect to interact in strange new ways.

Fortunately, the issues that precognition or clairvoyance raise for practically every scientific discipline need not concern us here, but the evidence of consciousness being able to "stretch" both through space and time does warrant such questions as, *"Does consciousness truly reside in the brain?"* Again, the evidence seems to imply that the brain is merely the focal point of a consciousness that does not adhere to space or time in the ways we have come to expect. But this is a discussion best saved for the end of this chapter. Instead, one of the most telling sessions will be briefly recounted below, so the reader might better understand both the process of remote viewing as well as the significance of its results.

A View Through Time

Though most of the early experiments remain classified, enough material has been made available to the public to prove some of the finer points of both the process and accuracy of remote viewing. Several research institutions with a more scientific objective have also evaluated the method since the cold war, finding substantial evidence that remote viewing can indeed provide reliable information.

Perhaps the most remarkable case, in both scope and accuracy, dates back to 1979. The National Security Council (NSC) asked the most consistently accurate of the army's remote viewers, an officer by the name of Joe McMoneagle, to *"look into"* a puzzling building somewhere in northern Russia that had recently showed up on spy-satellite photos. The photo had shown heavy-construction activity around the building, which was located a hundred yards from a body of water. The purpose of all this was a complete mystery to the NSC, which prompted them to turn to remote viewing for clues. Joe McMoneagle was given no information about this, of course, other than the map coordinates, yet managed to describe a cold location with large buildings close to a body of water, together with impressively accurate illustrations of the target area. As this material corresponded with the spy-photo, the officer in charge showed it to him and asked what was inside the building. McMoneagle described a large and active working area, where some kind of heavy construction was going on. In a later session he stated that a submarine was being built, which he sketched with some detail (including a long flat deck, strangely angled missile tubes, a double hull and a new type of drive mechanism). The strange shape and the enormous size—much larger than any submarine either NATO or the Soviet Union had at the time—along with the fact that the supposed construction was taking place so far from water, led the NSC to assume that he must be mistaken. No other sources of intelligence had indicated that anything of the kind was going on, which added to their scepticism, but McMoneagle's track record was too impressive to ignore. Therefore, he was asked to view the future, month by month, and report what he found. This he did, sensing that construction would be completed some four months into the future, and that a tunnel would be blasted from the building to the water, allowing the submarine to be launched. Four months later, in January 1980, spy-satellite photos showed this very process as the largest submarine in the world (eventually named *Typhoon*) travelled through an artificial channel from the building to the body of water, bearing a distinct resemblance to sketches from months earlier.[4]

Though one of the most lucid and demonstrative cases of remote viewing, and one that might take a moment or two to fathom, it is not the only such case. And even if it was, anyone arguing the "pure luck" alternative would be unlikely to meet with much success. Here we have a case of one mind describing uncannily correct and significant details about one of the most secret projects of the cold war era. One "rational" explanation would be that McMoneagle was in fact a high-ranking spy for the Russians with detailed information on their most secret projects. Or could it be that the NSC was *riddled* with Russian spies? These farfetched alternatives might appeal more to the reductionist point of view than the ESP alternative, but again, this was no isolated incident. The method has been evaluated at the Princeton Engineering Anomalies Research Laboratory as well as by other reputable institutions, resulting in overall odds against chance of 100 billion to one.[5]

Evidentially Psi

Several other successful studies into telepathy, clairvoyance and precognition have been conducted by a number of institutions, almost always arriving at the same conclusion: that these phenomena are scientifically valid. In some of these studies, the nervous system of the subject has been observed to react to imagery moments before the subject is actually confronted with the imagery in question; in other cases, successful attempts have been made to use psi to predict the behaviour of the stock market and much more. It all makes for very interesting reading if nothing else, and I would again like to recommend Dean Radin's book, *The Conscious Universe*, which reports extensively on this research. But for our purposes, it is enough to conclude that our minds can and do communicate with other minds as well as being able to gather information virtually unhindered by space or time. It should be obvious to anyone prepared to accept the scientific method that consciousness is much more than the mere firing of neurons within the brain. So what does all this mean?

In or Out of Mind?

ExtraSensory Perception, though it may to some degree answer such questions as what will happen at a specific location in the future, on the whole gives rise to a host of new questions. Does the mind "tap into" some field of emotional and factual information or is this "field" itself to be regarded as a living, autonomic consciousness? More puzzling, perhaps, how does the remote viewer "home in" on the right target with only map coordinates to go by, which sometimes never leave the sealed envelope they come in. Does the mind somehow sense not only aspects of the remote location, but also which location to visit? Clearly the "unknowns" outnumber the "knowns," with the only intellectual comfort being the fact that these "knowns" are acquired through careful scientific method and are statistically sound facts.

On the other hand, it should be remembered that science does not explain the *nature* of things, what things are, as much as their *function*, or how things work. ExtraSensory Perception works. Numerous trials of telepathy, clairvoyance and precognition repeatedly, and in different laboratories, produce results well over what is deemed statistically probable. But what ExtraSensory Perception actually *is*, well that is a completely different matter.

It seems that the notion of non-local mind is the best point of origin. Our mind, as we normally experience it, operates in the "here" and "now." Yet it seems that it can either "stretch out" or "gather in" impressions from sources distant in both space and time, which are then assimilated in the here and now.

There are many points to be made from this statement. Firstly, it seems fair to conclude that telepathy, precognition and clairvoyance are all basically the same phenomenon, in that they are expressions of non-local mind. That we divide them into subgroups is merely part of our scientific methodology: striving to understand the whole through examining the parts. We also divide them in this way as our ordinary consciousness (our "local mind," as it would now seem) sees these aspects as fundamentally different. After all, whatever Einstein and later physicists might have claimed about the true nature of space-time, we do not experience time and space as the same thing, even if we readily accept that all things must be located in both time and space in order to exist. Secondly, stretching out with mind (i.e., partially existing outside the confines of brain and cranium) implies something different from gathering information *into* mind.

If we are indeed reaching out with our minds then at least part of our consciousness is capable of leaving our body, which has implications for our spirit and its possible survival beyond death. Though *beyond body* is not, as we shall see later, the same as *beyond death*, it is undeniably an important step on the way. It is a step much as psychokinesis, the mind-matter link, was a necessary step for our soul to have a reason to exist at all. Gathering information into the mind, on the other hand, allows the limits of brain to remain intact. True, the two minds might actually be communicating telepathically, but for all we know telepathy may actually work along similar lines to that of radio waves, albeit non-locally and thus instantaneously. Thoughts may travel through this non-local "field" and be picked up by receivers in the mind, much as with communication through the use of a radio senders and receivers. Though in this case time and space seem to be of little consequence, mind as we know it may still be snuggled comfortably into the cranium, much as radio exists inside its casing. After all, we do not presume that a radio reaches outside its various components in order to create sounds, it merely picks up what flows through it. This, in turn, could mean that when the brain dies, the mind ceases to exist, at least in the sense that we usually mean. To clarify: it could be argued that our thoughts, feelings and actions continue to exist, much as our genes continue to exist, but we as individuals, as focal-points of consciousness, cease to be.

So which of the two alternatives is the more likely one? Can our personality and awareness of self exist independently of our body much as radio waves exist independently of receivers, or is the sensation of existing as an individual as confined to our body as the radio receiver is to its casing? Can mind exist without body, or do we need a body to have a mind? This is impossible to answer given our limited knowledge of the psi-phenomenon at this point. This is hardly surprising, considering that most scientists are as yet too occupied dealing with the strange fact that psi exists at all to be able to comment with any confidence on its nature. Perhaps science, as we recognise it, is simply not able to encompass the strange world of ESP without reinventing itself. And even if the second alternative proved to be true—that mind only makes sense of signals that somehow travel non-locally through and are picked up by it—the survival of the individual consciousness would not be any less likely. To put it bluntly: if thoughts and emotions can exist independently, why should not the process that creates them, consciousness, also be able to exist independently? Or to pose the same question from another angle: what is the difference between a person's thoughts and emotions and a person's consciousness?

Consciousness, referring back to Descartes' *cogito, ergo sum*, is more than the mere process of thinking and feeling. It includes "awareness," being aware and also being aware of this awareness. As we cannot measure or experience any other awareness than our own, it seems that reasoning in this direction can only take us so far. Even if it is possible to experience the awareness of another, our experience will inevitably and ultimately remain part of our own awareness.

So does this mean that searching further along the line of minds reaching out of the body is futile? Not really, as validated claims of out-of body experiences would make a strong case for the mind's ultimate independence from brain and body. If the mind can be shown to move about while the brain is incapacitated, then maybe the finer points of "gathering in" as a radio receiver versus "reaching out" as an independent force mentioned above could be settled. Perhaps they are merely expressions of the same basic phenomenon, the separate meanings only aspects we find reasons to delve in from our local perspective in time and space. In a non-local context, any aspect relating to time or space, such as *reaching out* or *taking in* or even *moving around*, would appear pointless. So we shall move ahead, and in the next chapter examine the claims of the out-of-body experience, along with the intriguing Near-Death Experience.

Summary

Ganzfeld, remote viewing, and related experiments prove that not only emotional, but factual and sensory information, may exist outside the body and still reach the mind. Through reaching out with our minds, we can tap into a great "field" of knowledge containing ordinary and non-ordinary perceptual information. This field extends both into the future and the past, and we can mentally gather information from it or through it whatever the distance in space or time between us and the source of the information. How this field relates to our individual non-local consciousness, or indeed if such individuality is possible we cannot say. Is some aspect of our mind roaming free, independent of our brain, or are we merely "picking up" knowledge that exists everywhere.

To answer this question, we must seek evidence that consciousness can exist independently of the brain, preferably with the brain completely "shut down." If such evidence exists, the case for the survival of consciousness would appear very sound indeed. And if such evidence exists, it will be found within the research into the Near-Death Experience.

VII

THE BRIGHTER SIDE OF LIFE

N ear Death Experiences came to the attention of the general public as well as the medical community with Dr. Raymond Moody's best-seller *Life After Life*. Thanks to the fact that these experiences take place in a relatively controlled environment, where so much is known about both the current situation and the medical history of the patient, a sizeable caseload has accumulated for us to draw from. Since medical personnel usually conduct the research, evidence in favour of the afterlife found here stands a fairly good chance of being widely accepted. In fact, no other area relating to postmortem survival enjoys the respect and standing that the Near-Death Experiences does.

Perhaps the term "near death" itself is somewhat misleading. Being "near" death implies that one was merely in a dangerous situation which could have resulted in death but fortunately did not. So, before discussing the survival or not of consciousness beyond physical death, we should probably agree on what we mean by the term. This might seem to be a simple task but it is not, as the boundaries of death seem just as elusive as those of life as examined so far.

WHEN IS DEATH?

Physical or biological death may seem as obvious as it is final, but this is mainly due to most of us not actually being around when it happens. As a rule we encounter death at funerals, which are usually held days or weeks after the event of death actually took place. For some of us, the closest that we get to death might be a mummified body in a museum—someone who met death thousands of years ago. Others encounter death more closely as it occurs or mere minutes after it has taken place. Whatever the case, death usually presents itself as a final, irrevocable fact that one can do little in the face of. Dead is dead, full stop, end of story. Or at least the end of the story as we know it.

Pinpointing the actual time when death occurs or life ceases is another matter altogether. The time of death might not be the point when the heart stops beating of its own accord, but rather the point when the medical staff cease their attempts at restarting it. In other cases, a person may be pronounced dead despite the fact that the heart is beating, because the brain has ceased to function. Indeed, the absence of any electrical activity in the brain is one of the surest indications that the specimen in question is indeed no longer alive. To complicate things further, people who have been pronounced dead do, on occasion, return to life. Simply put, though we in hindsight can tell with great certainty if a body is dead or not, the actual moment death takes place, or life leaves the body, is a tricky business indeed.

When a person returns to life, the scientific or medical conclusion is that the patient obviously was not dead after all, but only near death. The reason that they were *near death* rather than *dead* derives, at least in part, from the assumption that one does not return from death. The notion of death as an irrevocable fact, an end of the line finality, is embraced by medical personnel to the same extent as it is by everyone else. Though this might not have been the reason Raymond Moody coined the term in the first place, it is an interpretation of the term that most reductionists feel comfortable with. If people were actually *dead* they would not be having experiences, as death itself signifies the end of experience. An experience of death (involving tunnels, lights, spiritual beings and exceptional clarity of mind) would thus be a contradiction in terms. A clear-cut case of circular reasoning perhaps (i.e., incorporating the conclusion in order to arrive at it), but the simple philosophical truth is that we do not actually know. It is merely the traditional assumption of the scientific community that states that one cannot return from death because, under the ruling paradigm, death is the final state of the organism, after which it ceases to function and after which the illusion of consciousness is neither necessary nor possible.

The reductionist view, fundamental to the medical practice in the west, is not compatible with such concepts as the non-physical soul or consciousness existing without an animated and physical brain of some sort. True, the connection between mind and body is now widely accepted, but this connection runs both ways: no body, no mind. It should come as no surprise that much of the medical community regards tales *"from the other side"* with scepticism. After all, a person can survive short periods of "death"— where the brain is starved of oxygen due to the heart not pumping blood—with virtually no loss of mental capacity. However, the longer the brain is starved of oxygen, the worse the damage. Those who tell amazing stories after returning from brief periods of death always fall within the acceptable margin, generally returning without loss of mental capacity. After all, if this were not the case, the returning patient would not be able to tell the fanciful tale of his or her spirit leaving the body. Language and memory would be severely impaired and, in the worst case, the brain would be little more than a "vegetable."

The opposing view is, of course, that people returning from "death" to tell stories of the experience were *actually dead* and were indeed experiencing what life is like on the other side. Might not these "near-death" experiences be true "actual-death" experiences, rather than mere delusions of the dying mind? That they happen within the short period during which the mind may still be "reactivated" does not make the person less dead. If the person had not been reactivated, he or she would, after all, have remained dead in most cases. The mere fact that these experiences are short is not in itself a valid argument against their being actual and valid experiences of the "other side" (to use the popular phrase). They have to be short or the individual spirit would not be able to return to a functioning brain and body. Returning would simply be pointless if too much time had elapsed, it could be argued. From this perspective the preferred term might be "brief-death-experiences" rather than "near-death" ones. The accepted term, however, is "near death" and whether this term is correct or not, this is the term we shall use.

The answer to the question of when death actually takes place is like almost every other crucial question in this book impossible to provide. We have a pretty good idea of what death is, why it happens and what it results in for the body, but as Near-Death

Experiences show, the very moment of death (at least in an irrevocable sense) also boils down to a question of belief.

What Is a Near-Death-Experience?

Though most readers should be well acquainted with the phenomenon by now, a brief description is in order. The experience
usually starts with a patient in hospital or in a situation with medical staff present who can later attest that the patient was at least
briefly "dead." Obviously other cases exist, but without a quali-
fied witness around these cannot be classified as NDEs. More to
the point, perhaps, is that without skilled medical staff around,
the dead person is likely to remain just that. In the most common
NDE scenario, the patient's heart usually stops beating and the
medical staff attempt to get it going again. Up to this point, the
patient may have been anything from being totally aware and in
considerable pain, to being totally unconscious; but it is beyond
this point that things get interesting. All of a sudden the patient
will find him or herself "up in the air," looking down with calm
detachment at the body and the medical staff below, usually not
immediately realising whose body it is. Often the patient will later
be able to describe what was happening in the room with surprising accuracy.

After lingering or moving around a bit, a new development
might take place. Typically, the person will enter what is perceived to be a tunnel and travel at what is experienced as a
tremendous speed. Sometimes the person will encounter familiar
but previously deceased people along the way or perhaps beloved
pets that have passed away (common among children too young
to have lost many loved ones). Rarely, if ever, do they encounter
anyone still alive though, interestingly enough, several reports
exist of encounters with people believed to be alive but who in
fact had died, a fact that was not known by the person having the
NDE prior to the experience.

Eventually a light will appear at the end of the tunnel, growing
bigger as the person gets closer. This light might be accompanied
by alluring music and turn out to be a landscape beautiful beyond
description. Here the person will meet a being of light or deceased
friends and relatives, will often experience his or her life in full
review; and will often be offered the choice to stay or return. As

this new place is perceived as wonderful beyond words—as is the whole experience once the body is left behind—this will usually prove to be a tougher choice than might be expected. A symbolic barrier, such as a face or a gate, is often present, representing a point of no return. In still other cases the person is given no choice and is firmly ordered to return as he or she still has unfinished business in life. In some cases the person having the experience even has to plead with the being of light to return.

During the entire experience, the person feels calm and joyful, with a feeling of love at its core. Often the person will experience a singular clarity of thought—understanding the world on a whole new level—and the experience will feel more real than the reality left behind. Eventually, of course, the person will return to his or her body to tell the tale.

Though each tale is different and few contain all aspects mentioned above, things seem to happen more or less in this order. For instance, one does not first meet the being of light, then go through the tunnel and then have an out-of-body experience. It should also be pointed out that not all near-death experiences are pleasant: some are truly terrifying, full of demons and other hellish aspects, and some contain elements of both. Also, both cultural background and personal beliefs seem to influence the experience (as it does the person's interpretation thereof). Still, as far back as these experiences have been reported, and independently of whichever culture they originate from, the experience remains basically the same. Different cultures and different eras come up with different common traits, but as a whole, the experience seems pretty consistent. This implies that the experience is partly universal and partly culturally influenced, yet always individual.

Triumph of Spirit or Delusion of Mind

As mentioned above, there are basically two different interpretations of the near-death experience, the first being that it is merely a delusion of a dying brain, the second that it is our soul or consciousness disassociating itself from the dying or dead body. We shall briefly examine the arguments of the former interpretation, the mechanical or reductionist view, first.

Perhaps the foremost representative of this perspective is psychologist Susan Blackmore, whose 1991 book *Dying To Live*, makes

a very good case from an empirical point of view. She demonstrates how practically all the components of the near-death experience can be linked to different combinations of perfectly normal
functions of the brain. For instance, cortical disinhibition could
explain such visual effects as the famous "light at the end of the
tunnel." It has been argued that anoxia (oxygen starvation), leading to random excitation of the brain's neurones, could result in
such aspects as the life review. Heightened levels of carbon diox-
ide have been reported to result in several familiar aspects of the
NDE, such as the bright lights and the feeling of "more real than
reality itself." Endorphins, a natural substance similar to mor-
phine, are commonly released when a person is in pain, and can
produce various effects including lowering the threshold for
seizures in the temporal lobe. Seizures in this part of the brain
have been shown to be connected with religious or mystical experiences. That people have out-of-body experiences and feel de-
tached should not be surprising as this is, to some degree, common in threatening situations. So is the feeling of peace in people
who experience a narrow escape from death, even if they are not
actually harmed physically.

That people accurately describe conversations and procedures
that they "couldn't possibly be aware of" is explained by the fact
that they might well have been subconsciously aware of them.
(For instance, it is not uncommon that patients undergoing
surgery can still hear the medical staff's voices). Later the patient
mentally creates the out-of-body experience to describe what they
believe they actually experienced from above. The out-of-body
experience itself can be induced both electrically and chemically,
and is occasionally reported by patients returning to consciousness as the effects of such anaesthetics as Ketamine wear off—
patients who, it should be pointed out, were *not* near death in any
way during surgery. The similar aspects in all NDEs can be
attributed to physiological aspects of the process and the differences, cultural as well as individual, can be attributed to the psychological and cognitive makeup of the patient.

That the different aspects of the NDE can, to varying degrees,
be experienced in other traumatic and taxing situations, however,
does not mean that all these fragments will create an astoundingly
convincing and coherent whole in the dying brain. Indeed, from
the layman's perspective, it seems quite unlikely that such a jum-

ble of different experiences should be combined into anything coherent at all by the dying brain, but for supporters of reductionism such a process is far more likely than that the NDE should be evidence of a soul that can separate from the body. Such a notion would not only require a complete remodelling of the contemporary scientific paradigm, but would also demand a creation of completely new worlds where consciousness would go after death. Understandably, *Dying To Live* is held by many as definitive evidence in favour of a materialist perspective, that the near-death experience is merely the final illusion of the brain, consciousness being a mere illusion to begin with.

Fortunately for us, as we try to solve the mystery of consciousness, the material and insight provided in *Dying To Live* does not have to prove an obstacle. Firstly, as the brain and consciousness are clearly connected with each other, physiological aspects are only to be expected. We tend to get *causation* and *correlation* mixed up as we try to explain what causes what. For instance, do changes in the brain cause paranormal experiences or is it vice versa? Perhaps changes in our consciousness produce changes to the brain's activity? Perhaps electrical stimulation to the temporal lobe actually provokes a detachment from one's body, not merely the sense of detachment?

Any supporter of the contemporary scientific paradigm will, of course, dismiss this as ridiculous on the grounds of impossibility. But the scientific paradigm must change if it no longer can satisfactorily explain empirical evidence such as the observations reported in this book so far.

Since the reductionist paradigm cannot explain the non-local and universal aspects of consciousness, it should perhaps not be expected to explain more than the rudimentary aspects of the NDE. This prompts us to consider alternative explanations that encompass the new data on consciousness. Before we attempt this, however, there remains some relevant empirical evidence to examine, lending credibility to the hypothesis that the NDE is more than a mere delusion of a dying mind.

A BIRDS-EYE FOR DETAILS

While gathering information for her book, Susan Blackmore was unable to find any case that could convincingly validate the claim that the NDE has paranormal aspects. Naturally, stories abound of people seeing and hearing things they could not possibly have become aware of by use of natural senses, but stories need to be validated if they are to serve as evidence of anything other than humankind's proficient imagination. Fortunately, there are several interesting stories that have been validated, the most famous of which is probably the case of Maria's tennis shoe, a firsthand account of which was published in 1995,[1] and which is worth recounting here.

In this case, Maria, a migrant worker, experienced a partial NDE in Harborview Hospital in Seattle after suffering a cardiac arrest. Kimberly Clark, a critical care social worker, visited her the following day at which point Maria described having had an out-of-body experience in which she found herself floating above the hospital. Among other things, she remembered having seen a tennis shoe on a ledge outside one of the hospital windows. Maria not only was able to indicate the whereabouts of this oddly situated object, but was able to provide precise details concerning its appearance, including that its little toe was worn and one of its laces was stuck underneath its heel. Upon hearing Maria's story, Clark went to the location to see whether any such shoe could be found. The shoe was there as Maria had described it, except that, from the window, the details that Maria had specified could not be discerned. Upon its retrieval these features were confirmed. Clark concluded: "The only way she could have had such a perspective was if she had been floating right outside and at very close range to the tennis shoe."

This is not the only case of its kind. Dr. Kenneth Ring and Madeleine Lawrence have studied several cases where witnesses have corroborated information gathered during the out-of-body experience. The following cases are from Kenneth Ring's paper published in the *Journal of Near-Death Studies*.[2]

In one of these cases, also involving a shoe, a resuscitated patient recounted an NDE to Kathy Milne, a nurse at Hartford Hospital who had an interest in such experiences. The patient described floating out of her body, briefly viewing the resuscitation effort and then felt herself being pulled up through several floors of the hospital, ending up above the roof. Here she recognised the skyline of Hartford and also saw a red object on the roof which she identified as a shoe. The out-of-body experience then proceeded into a fairly typical NDE. Milne later told this story to a sceptical resident, who got a janitor to let him out onto the roof where he indeed found a red shoe.

A second case was reported by Joyce Harmon, a surgical intensive care unit (ICU) nurse at Hartford Hospital. Upon returning to work after a vacation, during which she had purchased a pair of plaid shoelaces she happened to be wearing that day, she was involved in the successful resuscitation of a patient. The following day she met the patient by chance, whereupon the patient immediately recognised her as the nurse wearing the plaid shoelaces on the day before. Though undetectable by someone lying in bed, the patient had apparently seen them while out of body and looking down from above.

In a third case Sue Saunders, a respiratory therapist at the Hartford Hospital, was helping to resuscitate a man in the emergency room whose electrocardiogram had gone flat. Medics were administering repeated shocks with no results, while Saunders attempted to give him oxygen. In the middle of the resuscitation, someone else took over for her and she left. A couple of days later, she encountered the patient in the Intensive Care Unit where he spontaneously commented: "You looked so much better in your yellow top." The man recognised her, was correct about her wearing a yellow smock as well as a mask while trying to give him oxygen, despite the fact that he was unconscious and without a heartbeat during her entire presence.

Another relevant case concerns a 41-year-old woman[3] who underwent a biopsy in connection with a possible cancerous chest tumour. Due to a mistake during surgery, her superior vena cava had been severed. She was rushed from the recovery room on a gurney to have an angiogram. Unfortunately the attendants slammed her gurney into a closed elevator door at which point the woman had an out-of-body experience. Apart from being able to see her own body beneath her, she could see down the hall where two men she knew were both standing, looking shocked. Though one of these men was unable to recall the incident (some years had passed when the facts of this case were gathered), the other was able to independently confirm all the essential facts of this event. This case is interesting for two reasons. Firstly, the respirator on her face obscured her field of vision, preventing the kind of lateral vision necessary for her to view these men down the hall.

Secondly, the inadvertent cutting of her superior vena cava caused a variety of medical catastrophes, including blindness. In other words, she was in all likelihood already completely blind when this event occurred. This leads us to another interesting area of research, near-death experiences of the blind.

DYING TO SEE

According to the materialist view a case that would constitute proof of the NDE's "supernatural" nature would be one in which a blind person correctly reported verifiable visual impressions during the experience. The argument behind this is that if our soul indeed leaves our body at death, gathering information by senses other than those provided by the body, blind people should have experiences more or less identical to those who can see. On the other hand, if the NDE is merely a constructed illusion of the dying mind as it assimilates residual information from the surroundings by "natural" means, visual data should not be a part of this experience. Presumably, any out-of-body elements to the experience should be auditory rather than visual.

The book, *Mindsight,* by researchers Kenneth Ring and Sharon Cooper, deals exclusively with the near-death experiences of blind people. More than 30 people were interviewed at length during a two-year study of near-death and out-of-body experiences in the blind, and the stories they tell make a convincing case for sight in the blind. In fact, the NDEs of blind people seem, on the whole, indiscernible from those of people who have no problem whatsoever with their sight. This includes both those who became blind later on in life as well as those blind from birth. Yet they generally provide visual recollections as clear as does everyone else when describing the out-of-body experience: the tunnel, the beings of light and so forth.

One such experience is that of Vicki, a 45-year-old woman who had been born blind. Following an automobile accident, she found herself floating above her body in the emergency room of a hospital watching a male doctor and a female nurse working on her body. She did not recognise herself at first, but identified the body as her own due to its design and the fact that she was wearing a "plain gold band on my right ring finger and my father's wedding ring next to it." Eventually she found herself going up through the ceilings of the hospital rooms until she was above the roof of the building. There she experienced a brief panoramic view of her surroundings. From this point she was sucked head first into a dark tube, yet she was aware that she was moving toward light. Upon exiting this tube, she found herself lying on grass, surrounded by trees and flowers and a vast number of people. Everything seemed to be made of light, not only a light one could see, but a light one could actually *feel*. Before returning, Vicki also experienced a complete panoramic review of her life, accompanied by an understanding of the significance of her actions and their repercussions.

Another case is that of Brad, also blind from birth, who had an NDE at the Boston Center for Blind Children in 1968 when he was eight years old. Brad's heart stopped for at least four minutes during a case of pneumonia leading to severe breathing difficulties, and CPR had been required to bring him back. During the experience, he saw his own body as well as his roommate who got up from his bed and left the room to get help. Brad experienced going through the ceilings of the building until he was above the roof, where he realised that he could see clearly. Here he identified the sky as cloudy and dark and saw snow everywhere except for the streets which had been ploughed (there had been a snowstorm the day before). He was able to describe the snow banks the ploughs had created, and gave a detailed description of the way the snow looked. He also recognised a playground used by the children of his school as well as a nearby hill he used to climb. As the experience progressed, he found himself in a tunnel and eventually emerged into a field illuminated by a tremendous light. Here he walked on a path surrounded by tall grass, and reported seeing tall trees with immense leaves.

Apparently, visual perception of the physical world can, at first, be both disorienting and disturbing to the blind. Vicki, for instance, had a hard time relating to it initially, as she had never experienced anything like it. Eventually, though, it became perfectly natural. But there is another important aspect here: the authors named the book *Mindsight* because the visual experience is not quite like seeing in the ordinary sense. Rather, it was described as a more *tactile* experience, as if seeing with the mind, rather than with the eyes. Brad described it as "feeling with the finger of his mind." He felt that he became aware of images in a way he did not really understand. This is interesting as visual impressions during the out-of-body experience should be expected to be different if these experiences indeed represent dislocated consciousness. After all, we are not seeing by normal means, whereby information on our retinas is conveyed to the sight centre of our brain and there constructed into an image. We see (if we see at all) with our minds, experiencing the physical world (and possibly a fraction of the afterlife) in a state of disembodied consciousness.

Nor is the use of "new" senses restricted to the blind as deaf people also report being able to hear during NDEs.[4] Dr. Melvin Morse has interviewed dozens of deaf children and adults who report hearing "in their minds." Many of these deaf children have some rudimentary hearing and report that the "hearing" during the NDE is very different than ordinary hearing. Dr. Morse argues that "sight" in the blind and "hearing" in the deaf is only to be expected, as the near-death experience is mediated through the right temporal lobe, and all the "seeing" and "hearing" is done through remote viewing and telepathy. It is the right temporal lobe that makes sense of "ordinary" input (be it visual, auditory, tactile or through some other normally available sense), so why should it not make sense of "extraordinary" input in the same manner? One child Dr. Morse spoke with described it as "sort of like floating out of his body, but sort of like walking into his mind."[5]

MIND-PERCEPTION

If we are to accept the notion that consciousness indeed separates from the body during the NDE, it seems reasonable to assume that all who experience such phenomena acquire information about their surroundings while out-of-body through the same kind of process. After all, we cannot bring our eyes and ears along while "we" float off, leaving our body behind. Hardly surprising, this is the natural argument against the validity of both the near-death and the out-of-body experience. How can a person see and hear without the use of the sensory organs designed for this task?

Clearly this is impossible according to the present physical and biological paradigm of sensory processing, so these experiences must be delusions. But, paradigms are logically inferior to empirical data. When new data presents itself which cannot be reconciled with the current paradigm, as is the case with most of the data in this book, old paradigms, must be expanded or discarded. As most people look at life through the bias of their own paradigms it is not surprising that the sensory input during the NDE is perceived as ordinary sight and sound. This is, after all, what most of us are used to and comfortable with. Even if we experience our surroundings by means other than ordinary, we are likely to translate these into terms we are familiar with. Therefore only those who are not accustomed to these "ordinary" senses are likely to react to it as something new or different. A parallel can perhaps be drawn to when we dream. Obviously we do not see, hear, feel, smell or taste anything in the normal sense of these words. Still, we are usually convinced that this is the case while dreaming, perhaps because our logical abilities are commonly impaired along with our sense of what is rational. The point is that we do not perceive reality as it is, but through our own set of biological and personal variations and limitations, and quite often we will not become aware of things we do not expect to become aware of.

From the above-related cases it is evident that there is more than meets the eye as far as near-death experiences are concerned, but can they be said to constitute proof that our individual consciousness survives the death of the body? Unfortunately, no, they cannot. Though they make a convincing case for non-local consciousness, it may still be argued that these experiences are merely made possible due to some residual activity in the brain. In other words, our non-local consciousness can still be linked to our ordinary consciousness, which might still be active even though our heart may not be beating. This no doubt sounds farfetched, but to be sure that mind can exist without brain we need evidence in the form of an NDE where the patient is by all medical standards "dead." Where both the heart is stopped and, more importantly, the brain is completely devoid of electrically measured mental activity. With all measurable forms of consciousness non-existent, will a patient still be able to accurately describe what is going on around him or her? Such a case would indeed be very indicative of the ability of consciousness to survive and function on its own accord, without a brain to support it.

Mind Without Brain

One case that approaches this physiological state was reported by Dr. Michael Sabom in his book *Light and Death*.[6] A 35-year-old woman had an NDE during an extreme form of neurosurgery called "hypothermic cardiac arrest" that has been developed to allow operation on aneurysms deep in the brain. Prior to surgery her eyes were taped shut to prevent them from going dry, and headphones were placed over her ears to prevent her from hearing anything but constant beeps. The purpose of these beeps was to monitor the responsiveness of her brainstem; electrodes had been fastened to its auditory section. Her body was then cooled to 58 degrees Fahrenheit, which lowered her metabolic rate enough to let the surgeons operate for a relatively long time deep in the brain. Her blood was then diverted from an artery to a heart-pump, which allowed the heart to be stopped. When the EEG was flat and the brainstem stopped responding, they shut off the pump and tilted the operating table so that all the blood would be drained out of her brain. Only then, when she was by practically every medical standard dead, was it safe to perform the complicated surgery on the aneurysm. The procedure was successful, but coming out of the surgery she had a cardiac arrest and had to be shocked twice for her heart to start beating on its own.

Upon recovery, the woman was able to give an accurate description of the process from an out-of-body perspective. She described both visual aspects, such as the highly specialised tools of the surgeon, as well as auditory information in the form of dialogue between the medical staff. Unfortunately it seems that the only corroborative evidence she was able to provide from an out-of-body perspective took place while her brain was at least partially active. Interestingly, the next stage of the NDE, the tunnel, light and encountering of dead relatives, seems to have taken place during the part of the surgery when the brain was devoid of both electrical activity as well as blood. Though this in itself may be considered a powerful indication of consciousness without a functioning brain, from a strictly empirical perspective it remains inconclusive. After all, we cannot objectively tell if this experience lasted for the duration of the brain's inactive state or if it happened in the split second before the brain ceased to function, yet was experienced as "timeless" or lasting.

For the sake of argument, let us presume that a case exists where the patient remains in an out-of-body state and is able to report objectively verifiable observations despite the brain's being completely inactive. Would this constitute the final evidence that consciousness can exist without a body? Though most scientifically disposed people would probably consider this to be convincing evidence, one might still, in the spirit of scientific inquiry and open-minded scepticism, argue differently. It is, after all, possible that such a patient might be completely unaware of what was happening while "out" or medically "dead," but upon returning to a normal state of consciousness the patient might tap into the field of non-local information, much as a talented remote-viewer would. Here, all information of what has passed (and presumably all that will come to pass) is available and could later be interpreted by their ordinary consciousness as an out-of-body experience taking place during surgery. A case of local consciousness tapping into non-local consciousness in order to fool itself into believing that it actually can retain its ordinary faculties even without a brain.

Though this explanation will probably strike most as highly esoteric, it is clearly a possibility, seeing how linear time as we understand it does not apply to non-local consciousness any more than it does to quantum processes. It also fits with the notion of the personal perception and interpretation theory presented above, in the sense that paranormally acquired information will be "translated" into familiar terms. Of course, the same argument holds true for a genuine NDE, so this will not tip the balance either way. Scientific reasoning can only take us as far as the evidence permits, and this seems to be the end of the line, at present.

SHAVING BY OCCAM

The argument that the dying person taps into the same energy that the remote viewer uses is known as *superpsi*, and it should come as no surprise that this notion originates from the field of parapsychology itself. Basically it states that any proof of the afterlife that is uncovered from the "other side" (such as mediums apparently receiving information from dead relatives), might actually be cases of exceptionally successful but subconscious psi. For example, it is impossible to tell whether a dead relative is actually being "channeled" through a medium, or whether the medium is unwittingly tapping into the sitter's knowledge and expectations, and answering accordingly. That the medium seems to know everything the dead relative knew and communicates with their expressions and mannerisms, it might actually be a case that in the trance-like state the medium is reading the minds of the living rather than the dead. Following the same lines, superpsi could arguably be the case with even the most convincing NDE, as demonstrated above. This would also seem to be the eternal problem of scientific method. From the philosophical standpoint we can know nothing for certain. From Socrates to Hume, the theme that we can prove nothing remains a fundamental discord in the harmony science attempts to reveal. Methods of dealing with this lack of certainty have been proposed by many philosophers.

One of the most popular methods was supplied by William of Occam in the 14th century who stated that: "It is vain to do with more what can be done with fewer."[7] This is generally taken to mean that one should opt for the simplest explanation, or the alternative that demands the least hypothetical or unknown aspects to be acceptable. *Occam's razor*, the name this popular maxim goes under, is generally used to slit the collective wrists of all things parapsychological by the defenders of rationality. In these cases, the argument goes as follows: why invent/suppose a whole new world when this world is sufficient to explain such phenomena. A good point, to be sure, but as we have seen, the contemporary paradigm is no longer plausible if we are to trust the integrity and intelligence of the researchers referred to here. The battle to be fought with Occam's razor in the present case is between *disembodied consciousness* and *superpsi*. So, which of these would appear to be best equipped to explain these remarkable feats of consciousness? Which one demands the least metaphysical stretch, is simpler, "can do with fewer"?

Personally, I side with those arguing disembodied consciousness as this seems to require "less" in Occam's terms. It strikes me as a fairly straightforward explanation. As it stands, it requires only the assumption that consciousness can exist without a body much as it can exist inside the body. From what we can tell, empirically speaking, consciousness is capable of both influencing the material world and extending well beyond the limits of our cranium. If it can do this, it seems a small leap of faith to assume that it should be able to sustain itself independently of the body. Granted, the experience of said individual consciousness is bound to be different, as NDEs indeed seem to support, but a sense of individuality and personality does appear to remain intact. These arguments could also be forwarded to support the superpsi alternative, but here more is required. This alternative demands that every aspect of everything past, present and future from the lives of galaxies to quarks should be stored somewhere for apparently no other reason than to fool us into believing we have a soul or are individuals. The person in contact with this field of eternal information remains temporal, remains part of the here and now, as it were. When they go, every aspect of their consciousness continues to exist in this field for some reason, as it presumably always has done as linear time does not apply here, but they, as individual sources of consciousness do not. A metaphysical version of the blueprint, if you will. It strikes me as strange that the universe should go to so much trouble to preserve information about every aspect of itself for no purpose at all, or at least for no purpose that makes any sense to us as individuals. On the other hand, from the materialist perspective, this makes complete sense as the universe serves no purpose in any case: the universe simply *is*. If it chooses to record every aspect of its existence in some esoteric way, then so be it; a recording is less of an ontological mystery than is the original phenomenon, at least by my reckoning. I am reluctantly compelled me to admit that my arguments are in no way sufficient to rule out the superpsi theory in favour of disembodied consciousness.

As it seems that Occam will be unable to settle the score (even if we were to ask him through a spiritual medium), it is best to stick with Socrates if for no other reason than that this allows for an open mind. An open mind is particularly important as we leave the world of the living behind and explore empirical evidence of spirits returning from the world of the dead; this might shed further light on the superpsi versus disembodied consciousness controversy.

CONCLUSION

The near-death experience is widely regarded as the most compelling evidence for life after death, not only by the general public but by many healthcare professionals and scientists. Still, this opinion is by no means shared by all, and many researchers prefer to explain the experience in terms of physiological causes. Though it is true that most aspects of the experience can be explained by biological and psychological means and some can even be replicated in laboratories, on the whole, reductionism falls short of a satisfactory explanation of the phenomenon. Reports of sight in the blind and hearing in the deaf during NDEs as well as "paranormally" acquired knowledge or conscious activity in brains that, by all medically accepted standards, should be "out cold" cannot be explained by these means.

In the light of the evidence available at the present time, two possible alternatives present themselves: *disembodied consciousness* or *superpsi theory*. While disembodied consciousness seems to be the most likely alternative, the superpsi theory cannot be ruled out.

Though we have come closer to our goal of proving that we have a soul which reveals itself to us in the guise of consciousness that survives the death of our body, we have yet to uncover conclusive evidence. As we have exhausted the research available to us on this side of death's partition, we must now look further, to the other side as it were. Does there exist any physical evidence of consciousness actually "passing over"? Not for brief periods of time as with the near-death experience, but for good (at least in regards to the previous body, that is). This is the topic of the following chapter.

VIII

SPIRITS ON THE REBOUND

R eincarnation is a popular religious theme. It is a fundamental mechanism in Buddhism and Hinduism, a component of many ethnically influenced Christian and Muslim traditions around the world, as well as an accepted theological hypothesis in a number of other religious practices. It is also possibly the most popular post-life expectancy theme of the diverse New Age movement, and as a general philosophy it seems to be on the rise, treated as an interesting hypothesis among agnostics in general. It seems that the notion that we have been around before and will return again appeals to us: it gives us a sense of continuity and reassures us that what we did not learn the last time around we will be given ample opportunity to learn this time or the next. Metaphysically speaking, reincarnation answers a lot of questions quite pointedly that non-reincarnation is hard put to explain: Who we are, why we are in the situation we are in, what we should do about it (i.e., learn) and where we are headed, are quite neatly answered by reincarnation. True, what happens when we leave the wheel of rebirth is pretty much open to speculation, but as an intermediary explanation of our *raison d'être*, reincarnation is logically sound. It should be pointed out that logical soundness is not the same as truth, it merely means that reincarnation as a hypothesis is not self-contradictory.

Reincarnation also contains the added intellectual challenge to the personality that it, the personality, is only a temporary vessel of the soul. It may exist eternally, unlike the body, but after its tour in the physical world it must integrate itself with the greater whole. If one lifetime is but a day in the life of the spirit, what is one personality, one might ask. The notion that "we" are simply an aspect or a phase of some greater entity beyond our scope of imagination can be just as unsettling as it can be comforting.

Another reason for the allure of reincarnation is that it is a very down-to-earth sort of doctrine. The concept and its mechanism are easy enough to understand, which on the other hand might deter those who prefer more lofty and abstract theological alternatives. Given the down-to-earth nature of reincarnation, one might expect to find ample evidence of past life experiences in present personalities, which also seems to be the case. What, if anything, such experiences signify is, however, another matter altogether.

Evidence of Reincarnation

A number of cases have been offered up over the decades as evidence of reincarnation, almost all of them of an anecdotal nature. From the perspective of consciousness they are often quite fascinating, many of them quite accurate descriptions of what everyday life in historical settings is presumed to have been like. Indeed, most people who reveal past life memories during hypnosis tend to describe "ordinary" lives rather than fanciful descriptions of life as Cleopatra or Julius Caesar. Though such tales are interesting in their implications—especially as those reliving these presumed post-life memories rarely have any knowledge, historical or otherwise, of the times they find themselves describing—they offer no conclusive evidence of actual reincarnation. As has been amply demonstrated earlier on, looking into the past and coming up with reasonably accurate descriptions is a feat that non-local consciousness has repeatedly pulled off through remote viewing. Similarly, a past-life memory containing empirical data not known to anyone living at present and which could later be verified (such as a past-life memory of a hidden treasure that could be retrieved from its hiding place), could also be explained through non-local consciousness. Super-psi is an equally probable explanation as disembodied (or in this case, re-embodied) consciousness.

Transpersonal Therapy (the area of therapeutically-oriented psychology that operates under the assumption that personality might indeed continue to exist in a disembodied state and thus influence the psychology of the present personality), has demonstrated remarkable success in treating personality disorders that traditional therapy has been unable to alleviate. Often as not, the reliving of "past-life traumas" free the patient of his or her dysfunctional behaviour in the present life with surprising effectiveness: lifelong phobias and obsessions let go almost instantly after the past life memory has been experienced. Some have taken this as evidence of reincarnation. On the other hand, one might take this simply as evidence that "reincarnation therapy" and other transpersonal methods are remarkably effective, and leave it at that. Psychologically, it is quite possible for a person to subconsciously invent a past life experience to explain a present life phobia or obsession in order to consciously disassociate oneself from the cause of the problem, and then from the effect. That the mechanism could be enhanced by non-local consciousness should hardly be surprising.

Personally, I prefer the notion of reincarnation to the more mechanical operations of super-psi, but preferences, though they might influence reality, prove nothing. Empirical evidence of reincarnation is scarce and dubious at best and were it not for the remarkable work of Ian Stevenson, a Carlson Professor of Psychiatry and Director of the Division of Personality Studies at the Health Sciences Center, University of Virginia, reincarnation would not be addressed in this book. As it is, however, doctor Stevenson and his associates have compiled an impressive caseload of empirically based evidence in favour of reincarnation.

Biological Evidence Indicating Reincarnation

In many cultures oriented towards reincarnation, the tradition and folklore hold that birthmarks constitute a link to the previous life. When children are born, parents and relatives examine their bodies for marks that might offer information about who the child was in the previous life. The child might be identified as a dead relative or deceased sibling or perhaps a dignified tribal elder who has passed away. Of course, often the previous life of the child will not be identified at all as many children have no particular birthmarks or have marks that do not correspond to anyone familiar. This tradition has survived the test of time, and for the last three decades it would also seem to have survived the test of Ian Stevenson, who has dedicated his professional life to researching the phenomenon. To date, Stevenson and his associates have studied some 2600 cases, uncovering many where children have birthmarks or birth defects that indeed appear to correspond with the physical characteristics of the claimed previous life.

It should be noted that these are field-studies rather than laboratory studies, and the research is more similar in method to NDE-research than the studies conducted in controlled environments described in earlier chapters. In other words, only such cases of claimed reincarnation that have been brought to the attention of Stevenson and his associates have been examined. This is, of course, a quite natural state of affairs, but it also means that there are no real control groups to measure the effects against, nor any reliable statistics. Each case must be measured on its own merits, but thanks to the meticulous attention to protocol and detail by researchers in the field, the merits of the different cases are plainly revealed. Over the following pages we will look into the methods and results of this research, but for a comprehensive and enlightening description I warmly recommend Stevenson's book, *Where Reincarnation and Biology Intersect* (Praeger 1997).

Birthmarks and birth-defects are clearly empirical in as much as they can be measured, but this naturally says little of what they are evidence of. As the attentive reader may be aware, specific birthmarks are sometimes passed down from generation to generation. Thus, it is only to be expected that a child will be born with a similar birthmark to that of a deceased grandparent once in a while. As for the more anecdotal evidence of reincarnation, a child learning to speak in an environment where pictures, stories and other references to the dead relative are common, might well include identifying references to this person in his or her language in ways that the parents might willingly interpret as stories of a previous life. Needless to say, this is also a valid argument against reincarnation, as parents who want to believe their child is a particular reincarnation will naturally seize every opportunity to do so. After all, even the most rigorous of scientists and sceptics confuse facts and belief from time to time, so it is hardly surprising that hopeful parents occasionally—or perhaps more than occasionally—fall prey to this. If it were only a case of similar birthmarks within the same family, little scientific attention would have been paid to the phenomenon, but the birthmarks and occasional defects go well beyond that of simple, inherited skin conditions. In Stevenson's research, several such marks have been shown to correspond with injuries or wounds that the deceased—and now supposedly reincarnated person—acquired during the previous life. Indeed, in several of Stevenson's cases, these wounds have been directly related to the cause of that person's death. We will examine two such cases later on.

In some cultures, relatives go so far as to mark the deceased person's body to make identification simpler in the next life. Such *experimental birthmarks*, as Stevenson calls them, are usually simple, yet distinctive enough to recognise, and the corresponding symbols have been shown to turn up on infants in several cases.[1] It is also worth noting that in several of Stevenson's cases, the reincarnated person is often from outside the family, and sometimes the parents have no idea who the child might have been in a previous life until the child starts talking about that life.

THE IMPORTANCE OF BIRTHMARKS

There are, according to Stevenson, three reasons why birthmarks constitute evidence of singular importance in reincarnation research. First, they are objective, measurable and reliable. Where autopsy reports of the deceased person indicate marks that correspond to marks on the child, we have some very reliable evidence. We do not have to depend on informants' memories that may well be faulty; rather we have medical references as supporting evidence. Secondly, they lend strength to the idea that a deceased personality may influence the body of a new person. The non-local connection between consciousness and the physical among the living has been thoroughly researched, as reported in Chapter 3. In the case of birthmarks and defects, it would appear that consciousness of the no-longer "physically" living might also influence the physical world, or at least the bodies they are designated to inhabit. Here we would find some very compelling evidence that our consciousness survives physical death more or less intact. Though the superpsi option presented in the previous chapter may still explain some aspects of this process, I would argue that here we are dealing with spirits or souls (i.e., disembodied consciousnesses), as will be made clear later. Thirdly, these cases might, according to Dr. Stevenson, actually explain why some infants are born with birthmarks and defects despite the fact that the parents have no such marks. The cause of birthmarks and defects remain, in most cases, an unknown to modern science.

CASES OF REINCARNATION

To give the reader a better grasp of Stevenson's work, two cases will now be briefly presented, but I again urge those who are interested, especially those sceptically so, to read Stevenson's book for a broader and more thorough description of the field.

The first case is that of Ma Htwe Win, who was born in Burma in May 1973.[2] Prior to the child's birth, her mother had dreamed about a man she did not recognise; he appeared to be approaching her on his knees, or perhaps on amputated stumps of legs. When Ma Htwe Win was born her parents immediately observed that she had several birthmarks and birth defects. The fifth finger of her left hand was absent and she had prominent constriction rings around her left thigh and just above her ankles, much as if an imaginary rope had been tied there. She also had several distinctive birthmarks on her lower left chest in the region of the heart and on her head. Her parents had no explanation for these marks and defects, but were supplied with one when the child eventually began to speak. Ma Htwe Win claimed to have been a man called Nga Than who had been attacked by three men. She described how Nga Than had fought back, but unfortunately got his sword stuck in a wall, and had been stabbed in the left breast, had his finger cut off and was struck on the head. Ma Htwe Win then described how the assailants bound the body by tying the legs back on the thighs to make it easier to fit into a gunny sack, and then dropped it into a nearby dried-up well. Ma Htwe Win's statements proved to be correct, inasmuch as they could be verified as the life and subsequent death of a man called U Nga Than.

As it turned out, U Nga Than's wife, who had been a party to the murder and had claimed that he had simply left her and gone away, later married one of the murderers. While quarreling with her new husband, the facts surrounding the death of U Nga Than, including where the body had been disposed of, were mentioned. A neighbour happened to hear this and alerted the police who went to the abandoned well and found U Nga Than's body still tied up with the ropes that had been used to make it more compact. As it happened, Ma Htwe Win's mother, who had been two and a half months pregnant at the time, passed this well as she was returning to her village from the main road, and briefly saw the body and the ropes before she continued on her way. The dream mentioned above occurred the night following the incident.

In addition to her statements, Ma Htwe Win spontaneously recognised one of U Nga Than's murderers who was still in the area, and showed considerable fear towards him. She also recognised U Nga Than's son and asked her parents for money to give to him. Ma Htwe Win also showed some masculine traits, such as a wish to wear boys' clothes, and expressed a wish to revenge herself on U Nga Than's murderers. As for her birthmarks, the constriction rings of the lower legs matched those of the left thigh when her legs were bent backwards, but no data exists of exactly how the rope around U Nga Thang's body had been tied. Nevertheless, the description Ma Htwe Win gave was certainly consistent with her physical traits, and U Nga Thang's legs were indeed tied back after some fashion. This would also be consistent with the dream of the man walking on stumps.

The second case is that of Semih Tutusmus who was born in Turkey in 1958. Two days before his birth his mother had a dream in which a man by the name of Selim Fesli figured. In the dream, the man's face was covered in blood and he claimed to have been shot in the ear. He also announced that he intended to stay with the dreamer. A man by the name Selim Fesli had indeed been shot in the head at close range by a neighbour who was out hunting in the twilight. Though the shot had been an accident, the neighbour fled the scene fearing revenge from Fesli's sons. Eventually Fesli was found by villagers and taken to the hospital where he died some six days later. Though she had never met the man, she knew of him and knew vaguely about his death, but her husband had known the man well. When Semih was born his right ear turned out to be severely deformed, being little more than a stump, and the entire right side of his face was underdeveloped. Semih began to talk about the life of Selim Fesli at the age of one and a half. His first reference to the subject were the words "Isa Dirbekli" the name of the neighbour who had shot Selim Fesli, and then stated more details how he, as Selim Fesli, had been shot in the ear. He was able to correctly state the names of Selim Fesli's wife and six children, and recognised several people known to Fesli. The facts about Fesli's death were no secret, and it is possible that the child somehow learnt them through his ordinary senses, though this in itself would be an extraordinary feat for a child of one and a half. However, given his birthmarks and his singular identification with Selim Fesli—to the point of denying he was Semih Tutusmus at all—some non-local bond of consciousness between the previous personality and the present one cannot easily be ruled out.

Semih displayed a strong desire to be with the family of Selim Fesli: prior to the age of four he made his way to the village where the family resided, some two kilometres away, and introduced himself. He repeatedly visited the family and was reported to act much as the father of the family would, and was to a certain extent accepted as the reincarnation of Selim Fesli by the family. Also, Semih displayed an attitude of deep animosity towards Isa Dirbekli. Dirbekli had spent two years in prison for killing Fesli, but this seemed to do little to appease Semih, who threw stones at him when they met and openly threatened to kill him. Though Semih was still a child, Isa Dirbekli took these threats seriously and stayed away from the area where Semih lived. Resat Bayer, who worked with Stevenson in investigating this case, attempted to persuade Semih to adopt a more forgiving attitude, but this met with little success. Though the boy accepted the notion that he as Selim Fesli was alive again in Semih Tutusmus, therefore not dead at all and thus should not need to avenge himself on "his" murderer, the boy claimed he could not help himself. Whenever he saw Isa Dirbekli he could not prevent himself from wanting to throw stones at him and beat him up. This vengeful attitude continued to the age of 18, when Semih received plastic surgery during his military service resulting in a remarkably normal-looking right ear. The disappearance of his visual defects seem to finally enable him to give up his obsession for revenge on Isa Dirbekli, according to Stevenson.

It should be noted that, though both of these cases are fairly extreme as far as the physical defects are concerned, they are by no means unique. Neither are they unique in that the child identified with the recollected previous life, nor are they singular as to the amount of verifiable and correct information the children provided about the assumed previous life. Most cases, however, are less pronounced as far as the physical traits in the child go, and in some cases the physical anomalies take on such expressions as a different pigmentation or differently shaped eyes. Different from the child's family and parents, that is, but consistent with the previous life the child claims to have led. In addition to these physical traits the child will often display behavioural traits that are markedly different from his or her peers, but would be natural for someone of the culture of the previous life that the child identifies with. Finally, it should be noted that although in both these cases the parents had some knowledge and/or contact with the deceased personality (which might explain the child's knowledge of this claimed previous life), such a connection does not always exist. Stevenson reports at least 25 cases where the assumed previous life was identified and where the parents had no prior knowledge or contact with the deceased prior to this identification. Naturally, in many cases the "previous personality", to use Stevenson's expression, is never identified, making any verification impossible, but such is the nature of the research. The focus and point of interest of the research is to determine to what extent the child is factually correct about the previous personality, to what extent the physical anomalies of the child correlate to the wounds and other physical characteristics of the previous personality, and to what extent the behaviour of the child resembles that of the previous personality.

INVESTIGATING REINCARNATION

During the past three decades of investigation, Ian Stevenson and his associates have found that several features recur on a regular basis. The most interesting features from the empirical perspective are birthmarks and birth defects but, as noted previously, several other features occur on an occasional to a regular basis that might offer some clues of both the likelihood and mechanics of reincarnation. Cases of reincarnation are, much like with the NDE, culturally influenced and individually different, but basically conform to a similar, basic pattern wherever they occur over the globe. Some features are more common in some areas, other features dominate elsewhere, but the basic mechanism of the process of reincarnation, if this is indeed the case, seems universal. To get a better grasp on the mechanism of this presumed process, we will examine these features one by one.

The first feature, though uncommon, is that of an individual—usually an elderly one approaching death—who expresses a *wish* to be reborn to a particular couple. When a child is born with similar physical traits, it is often presumed that the child is the reincarnation. Predictions of this kind occur among the Tlingit of Alaska and the lamas of Tibet, but rarely among other cultures.

The second feature of a developing case is the *announcing dream*. In such a dream the deceased person appears, usually if not always, to the future mother and expresses his or her intent to be reborn into that family. Though the announcing dream occurs in most cultures, it is particularly common among the Tlingit of Alaska and the Burmese. Interestingly, such dreams usually occur before birth among the Tlingit, yet occur before conception among the Burmese. This, as Stevenson points out, is probably in line with the view of Burmese Buddhists that, when a soul attaches itself to an embryo, it can no longer communicate through such methods as dreams. Perhaps the minds of the living simply turn off the lines of non-local communication at this point due to their preconceived opinions, an interesting feature in line with the *mindset* argument to be explored later.

The deceased person is by no means always an acquaintance of the dreamer, nor is the dreamer aware that the person "visiting" her dreams is indeed deceased. Often the dream, even if memorable, does not make any sense until after the birth of the child. Though one might be tempted to dismiss the idea that a dead person could be communicating with the living through dreams, dream communication itself is not uncommon in parapsychological circles. The anecdotal evidence of precognitive dreams is vast and, if physicist Fred Alan Wolf is correct, the entire universe communicates through dreams.[3]

The third feature comes into play at birth, and consists of birthmarks, birth defects and any other visible aspects that may help identify the previous identity of the child. These visual attributes can represent any number of clues. Sometimes these marks will be identified as the gunshot wound that killed an uncle, and cases exist where birthmarks seem to mimic both entrance wounds and exit wounds in the appropriate location. Another time a malformed ear, such as was the case with Semih Tutusmus, or a missing limb will be identified as the resulting injuries to a friend or relative who was killed by robbers or run over by a train.

Sometimes the birthmarks and defects are larger or more encompassing than the presumed corresponding wounds that led to the previous personality's death, but in these cases the birthmark or birth defect can usually be connected to the lethal wound. For instance, if the previous personality died due to head trauma after being hit by a car, the burgundy coloured birthmark covering part of the child's face might well correspond to the haemorrhaging of the cranium. Stevenson mentions several cases of such birthmarks in which the common trait was that the body was not washed before it was cremated. If such a correlation does indeed exist, it has implications for how mind and body interact, but sheds little light on whether we are dealing with a disembodied personality or superpsi.

When researching birthmarks, it is required that at least one adult confirm that the birthmarks were present on the infant at birth or, at the very most, a few weeks after birth. An older child may have many marks that could be mistaken for birthmarks but were actually acquired later in life—even fresh insect bites can be confused with birthmarks. Only when marks can be confirmed as actual birthmarks can any acceptable comparisons be made to autopsy reports, photographs or reliable descriptions of the previous personality's physical features or wounds. (Of course, there are many cases of claimed reincarnation where no physical features exist, but these are not included in the research described in this chapter.)

The fourth feature occurs along with the development of speech in the child, and consists of the *reference* to a previous life. In rare cases the child will make physical references to the previous life before speech is developed, but these are not likely to make much sense until the child has developed enough vocabulary to explain itself. One such case was a child who remembered the previous life of a monk who was killed by a blow to the back of the head in a monastery not too far away. The child appeared to refer to this at an early age by patting the back of its head, which was slightly indented at birth, and pointing toward the direction of the temple. As it turned out, a monk had indeed been killed by a blow to the back of the head prior to this child's birth in circumstances similar to those described by the child.[4] Verbal references to a previous life usually occur, if at all, between the ages of two and four, though sometimes later. Most children who speak of a previous life do so with some intensity and emotion, and have trouble separating their past and present identity, when describing the previous life.

The fifth feature is *unusual behaviour* in the child. Unusual, that is, given the settings of the child's present situation, though perfectly logical if the child is indeed the reincarnation of someone else. Such was the case of the child who remembered the life of a murdered monk. For instance, the child would insist on sitting in an elevated position when the family sat down for a meal, rather than taking his place on the floor with everyone else. This behaviour was completely unsuitable for a child, but well in accord with how a monk accustomed to a superior position would behave.

It is also of some significance that the reincarnated person is often from outside the family, and sometimes the parents have no idea who the child might have been in a previous life until the child starts talking about that life.

FORMER LIFE IDENTIFICATION INTENSITY

The extent to which the child identifies with the previous personality will vary, but most of the time the identification is stronger than a mere "whim" or anything that can be attributed to chance. In mild cases, children have been reported to remark on a few aspects of the previous life, such as "I was a teacher when I was big" or "I was killed by a train." The child will not be obsessive about his or her previous life, but sufficiently open to help researchers find the previous personality. In the more extreme cases, the child will completely refuse to accept his or her current life. The child might insist on being addressed with the name of the previous personality, or may refuse to acknowledge his or her parents for who they are. In fact, if the child identifies with a previous life of a higher caste or level of society, he or she might treat the parents as servants. Generally, such a child will communicate from the standpoint of the previous personality, addressing with respect only those older or socially higher than the previous personality. The child may also display skills that it has not been taught by its present family but that the previous personality is known to have had. The child might even demonstrate such strange addictions, at least for a child, as a craving for tobacco or alcohol. If the child's previous personality was of the opposite sex, he or she may refuse to wear clothes of his/her "current" gender. The child may also demonstrate markedly masculine or feminine behaviour, depending on the previous life. Such cases as these, which vary from annoying to directly painful for the parents, suggest that the behaviour of the child is not due to intended or subconscious conditioning by the parents, but rather originates from some other source. If this source is a previous personality, as the child often claims, remains an open question.

Some children exhibit *phobias* that appear to stem from the previous personality. If death was due, for example, to snakebite, the child might have a phobia for snakes; if death was by drowning the phobia might be water; and if the previous personality was stabbed, it might be knives that the child fears. Phobias, nearly always related to the nature of the death of the previous personality, occur in roughly 35 percent of all cases reviewed by Dr. Stevenson. *Philias* (i.e., attractions) are also common, and usually correspond to the desires of the previous personality (e.g., the tobacco and alcohol mentioned above).

Of further note, if the child remembers being murdered in the previous life and meets the murderer in this life, the child will display great fear and almost invariably treat this person with severe and often unrelenting hostility. In many cases, the child will be obsessed with wanting to kill this person, much as was Semih Tutusmus, sometimes even going so far as attempting to do so. We shall examine this extreme behaviour and its implication later on.

Some cases exist where the child identifies so strongly with the previous personality that the 'new' personality is unable to develop freely. Occasionally the child will be unable to let go of the animosity towards those who caused the death of the previous personality, in other cases the family of the previous personality will have accepted the child as the reincarnation so fully that it has joined this family instead. Normally, though, the memories and the behavioural traits eventually fade. Interestingly, the behavioural traits last much longer than the memories of the previous life. That is, the child may stop talking about the previous life while still a child, yet may display behavioural traits well into the late teens.

It is interesting to note how often the child reports a violent death as the end of the previous personality. Violent deaths are reported in just over half of all the cases, though this varies greatly from culture to culture. In some cultures the rate drops to 29 percent, whereas in others it is as high as 74 percent, though in all cultures the rate is well above the average rate of violent death. Thus there seems to be a clear connection between violent deaths and birthmarks or birth defects in cases of reincarnation, though the exact nature of this connection is a matter of speculation. Perhaps it is as Stevenson suggests: that violent deaths make particularly strong imprints on the soul.

If the family of the previous personality can be located, the child will usually recognise parents, spouses, siblings, relatives and friends, often addressing them in a familiar way. At times the child will only recognise some people from the previous life and not others, which is a puzzling feature. This will often result in some members of the previous family accepting the child as the reincarnation, whereas others do not. In many cases, details about the previous life given by the child will be confirmed, and quite often the child will demonstrate the same preferences and aversions as the deceased person.

Though all the features above have occurred on several occasions, only four are so common that Stevenson names them as universal. These are: speaking about a previous life at an early age; ceasing to speak about a previous life at a later age (usually between 5 and 8); the high incidence of violent death in the previous life; and the frequent mentioning of this mode of death by the child.

ARGUMENTS AGAINST REINCARNATION

There are many arguments put forth against reincarnation, ranging from the mundane to the more esoteric. For instance, it is often argued that cases of reincarnation are merely fanciful interpretations enforced by wishful thinking in the parents. Though this no doubt is true in some cases, this does not explain those cases where birthmarks and birth defects are shown to be similar to those of the previous personality, at least in those cases where this personality was not known to the parents. Another argument is that parents attempt to influence their children, consciously or subconsciously, to take on the role of a deceased person for the benefits this might give the family. This is also probably true in many cases, but does not explain cases where the family has nothing to gain. Quite to the contrary, Stevenson can report several cases where the previous personality was more of a curse than a blessing. Another counterargument is provided by Dr. Erlendur Haraldsson[5] who has conducted a study into the psychology of children who remember what seem to be previous lives. The basic assumption is that children who conform to their surrounding expectations, subconscious or otherwise, and succeed in constructing a convincing imaginary personality, ought to be unusually sensitive to suggestion. Haraldsson's study showed no such heightened sensitivity in this group compared to their peers, which further implies that these children's tales of previous lives do not originate from conditioning in any traditional sense. The arguments for and against some kind of conditioning using non-local consciousness will be discussed later on.

Though it is difficult to apply statistics to cases of reincarnation, one can in each individual case evaluate the evidence as it stands, much as one would at a legal trial. If the subject can correctly describe significant aspects of the deceased's previous personality as well as the circumstances of their life, and is able to recognise friends and relations of the deceased, some connection must be conceded. If this connection cannot be explained by ordinary circumstances, we should definitely begin to assess the alternatives. If the subject also demonstrates some distinctive traits of the deceased, especially such traits as would be highly unlikely to find in a child, and the subject was born with equally distinctive physical features that correlate with wounds and other aberrations of the deceased, an alternative explanation to chance definitely requires some serious consideration. Naturally, in a population of over five billion people, quite a few children are bound to come up with fanciful tales that just happen to coincide with actual facts. Perhaps a handful of these will just happen to be born with birthmarks and birth defects that also happen to coincide with these facts, but how many cases do we require before we can allow ourselves to acknowledge that there must be more than meets the eye? On the other hand, given the empirical evidence of non-local consciousness, we have a far more workable concept to help us make sense of these anomalous occurrences, if they are indeed anomalous at all.

Recycled Souls or Recycled Thoughts

So are these actual cases of reincarnation facilitated by a disembodied consciousness? Though it may be tempting to make the leap of faith, to presume that reincarnation is indeed the only viable alternative, the super-psi hypothesis must still be evaluated. The evidence of non-local consciousness and its interaction with the surrounding world is abundant. Experiments with remote viewing demonstrate that nothing is truly secret, however private we might think it is. Experiments with cells demonstrate that these are privy to a surprisingly sophisticated level of consciousness and most medical doctors and psychologists will admit that the mind can influence the body to a great extent—religious stigmatism is one example of many. In light of this, the admirably tenacious sceptic might argue that what seems to be reincarnation is merely the developing consciousness of the foetus "tapping into" the non-local and timeless personality of someone deceased, identifying with this personality much as a plant would identify with its owner or caretaker. Perhaps the issue of violent death, linked as it seems to be to the cases of presumed reincarnation reported here, adds urgency or power to the imprint of the previous personality, making it easier to adopt for an evolving consciousness. So as the foetus develops into an infant, the second-hand experience of the violent death might result in physical birthmarks or birth defects. The imprints of the previous personality remain in the brain as memories and behavioural quirks that are later expressed by the child, but eventually the memories fade as the child's consciousness develops in its own right.

The fact that some birthmarks coincide with marks made on the body after death to help future identification, neither supports nor contradicts this possibility. If the child is indeed picking up and assimilating information through a process similar to remote viewing, it would be easy enough to "home in" on such information, specifically if the marks (such as experimental birthmarks) were made with the intent of later identifying the reincarnated personality. Actually, from what little we know, this would seem to support the super-psi alternative more than that of actual same-spirit reincarnation of a disembodied consciousness. Why, the argument can be stated, should a disembodied spirit be interested in the markings someone else places on the body after the spirit presumably has left?

There are, however, two arguments that can be made in favour of reincarnation over the assimilation of a previous consciousness by the evolving embryo. The first is that the field of consciousness possible for the foetus to tap into, via such methods as remote viewing, is non-local and thus not bound by time. If these cases constitute the mere assimilation of a deceased personality, as opposed to the actual continuation of a previous personality, then the reported cases should not follow time-bound causality as they do. In other words, children describing previous lives ought to describe lives from the future as well as lives from the more distant past. As it is, practically all the children interviewed by Stevenson and his associates describe lives of recently deceased people, the time of death ranging from weeks to at most a few years prior to their births. Also, it should be noted, a geographic proximity between the birthplace of the child and the place of death of the previous personality is an equally common feature.

The second argument is that the non-local field of consciousness where all the relevant information about the previous personality exists ought to be open to every evolving foetus. As this is the case, a multitude of children ought to assimilate this information, resulting in several children with similar birthmarks or defects and similar stories about the same previous personality. If violent deaths make especially powerful imprints on the field of consciousness, one would expect to find even more children assimilating this information than that of other previous personalities. Again, in almost all the cases examined, the previous personality does not seem to be a shared one. This does not mean that this does not happen, and Stevenson points out that such cases can not be excluded, but the rule so far seems to be that the previous personality only resurfaces in the consciousness of one child.

THE LANGUAGE OF REINCARNATES

A final and somewhat esoteric argument to be made against reincarnation is the fact that few children appear capable of speaking the language of the previous personality when this is different from the language the child is learning, a feature known as Xenoglossy.[6] For instance, Stevenson reports several cases of

Burmese children claiming previous lives as Japanese soldiers at the end of World War II. In these cases, however, the children spoke Burmese, not Japanese. These children would tend to refer to places, objects, preferences and cultural traits of the previous personality, as well as display behaviour compatible with a Japanese soldier rather than a Burmese child and sometimes referred to names, yet spoke to their parents only in Burmese. It could be argued that if these children truly identified with their previous personality, they would probably have refused to speak the Burmese tongue in the same way they refused to comply with Burmese custom, opting for the native tongue of their previous personality. After all, why should they not remember something as basic as language if they could remember so many other details and display so many cultural traits?

The answer to this enigma is most likely to be found in the nature of language. Where faces, objects, behaviour and places are mentally represented as themselves, language is, perhaps, of a more symbolic nature. That is, when we picture an object in our mind we "see" that object with our minds eye, but when we contemplate a word in our mind, we hold its meaning rather than its sound or the way it looks when written on paper. Language, spoken or written, is nothing more than a representation of the meaning of a word. I think that most professionals in the area would agree with me that a child generally learns the meaning of something (that juice comes from a container in the refrigerator) before it makes the connection between the sounds that represent the meaning (be it "juice," "container" or "refrigerator"). Later on, when the child has begun to understand words and grammar, the child may ask what a specific word means, but mentally we think in meanings and images, not words. A demonstrative example is the medical condition known as *aphasia*, where the patient has suffered damage to the language centre of the brain. Often the patient retains full mental capacity, but is somehow cut off from the language with which to express this capacity. So the patient may recognise a doctor or a nurse, know what their function or meaning is, but will be unable to translate this knowledge into words or symbolic behaviour. The patient might simply know how one beckons a person closer, how one asks for a drink or expresses any other desire, and so on. The patient might even be able to recognise the letters of a book, being well acquainted with the concept of reading, yet will have no idea what the words mean. Unlike waking up in a different country with a completely different language, the patient will in extreme cases even be unable to use basic sign language, and will only be able to express intent and emotion in the way a very small child would. Though it can be a horrifying experience to be mentally imprisoned in this way, fortunately many patients suffering from aphasia do recover to report on the evidence that meaning does indeed run deeper than language.

To conclude this line of reasoning, it is possible the child remembers the meaning of the previous personality's native tongue, but not the symbolic language itself. Simply put, language belongs to the biological brain whereas meaning is a property of consciousness. Meaning is the same for everyone, though language may differ. In the same way it seems to be meaning rather than words and figures that are communicated in remote viewing, ganzfeld telepathy and other experiments that employ our non-local consciousness. Indeed, in remote viewing, it has proved a lot easier to correctly identify concepts, such as 'humid', 'elevated', 'claustrophobic', 'intense' or 'peaceful' than specific words or series of numbers. As it comes naturally for the participant of these experiments to use spoken language to describe what he or she sees, feels or senses, it ought to come natural to the child to describe the previous life in the language that comes with the new body.

FROM THE CHILD'S PERSPECTIVE

If reincarnation is real, why is not the reincarnated child simply an adult in a child's body? Why does the child not have all the memories and skills and traits of the previous personality, and why does it not act like a miniature adult?

Answered simply, a child sees the world from a child's perspective. When we are children, we react spontaneously, are less emotionally inhibited and have a very different understanding of the world. Imagine having much of our personality and memories implanted in a child's body with a child's mind, vocabulary and emotions. Imagine further that this personality has to lie dormant until the child becomes old enough to understand the complex memories, emotions and thoughts which are the hallmark of this personality. It seems likely that all but the most dominant features would fade into the background, and as the child and the new mind grows older, identifying further with its present life, that even these dominant memories will eventually disappear too. After all, the new life of the developing child takes up most of its time, and the old has little to offer. Indeed, one might ask where the seat of consciousness is in such a split-personality case, as this must be. Perhaps the previous personality exists merely in the non-local part of consciousness, whereas the new developing personality resides in the local and personal consciousness linked to the physical brain. The more powerful the previous personality, the more it will be able to influence this new composite consciousness from its non-local position; but, in the end, it must be assimilated into the new personality—the new life—as consciousness cannot continue to function well when divided in this way. This seems to be the case, as children refer less and less to the previous personality as they grow older. The fact that behavioural patterns, such as Semih's resentment towards his "murderer", last longer than memories further support this notion. Perhaps when we are infants and before we develop a sense of self, we are more active in our non-local consciousness, gathering information we do not yet understand, in ways we adults, through experiments with non-local consciousness, have only begun to realise are possible. Perhaps it is as the poets say, that children cry because they know the secret of where they came yet lack the means to express it. Or perhaps they are just hungry, as the materialist would no doubt argue.

Be that as it may, based on what we now know about remote viewing and non-local consciousness, I would go so far as to say that reincarnation is the most likely explanation, with personality assimilation in second place and parental conditioning combined with wishful thinking a distant third. Other more anecdotal evidence, primarily from the area of transpersonal psychology[7], would seem to corroborate this view. Ian Stevenson also mentions spiritual possession as a possible, though not favoured, alternative. Possession is an interesting alternative to reincarnation, but ironically it matters little to us at this point, as both are by their nature equally supportive of our hypothesis: the postmortem survival of the human soul.

Comments on Karma

From a religious perspective Stevenson's research is more than slightly provocative, even if you are a Hindu or a Buddhist. After all, it does not really seem fair that a murdered person should have to be reborn with the physical defects that the murderers caused. The other way around would seem more just and appropriate, one would think. True, in some of the cases Karma seems to make some sense, as with Japanese soldiers being reborn into the Burmese families that they attempted to subdue during world war two, but on the whole there seems to be no direct spiritual justice overseeing the process in its infinite wisdom. On the other hand, perhaps we have simply misunderstood the essence of Karma and how it influences us.

We make many decisions and take many actions during life, resulting in material gain and loss, but most of the time it is our basic attitude that dictates how spiritually content we are. One thing may lead to another as causality still dominates the physical world, but it is our interpretation of that *one thing* or *another* that really limits or facilitates our happiness. Though most of us would not mind more money or more things, these material gains do not necessarily lead to more spiritual fulfilment, rather they bind us to the physical by distracting us from the spiritual. Still, we often appear to presume that when we die, we will quite naturally become perfect spiritual beings without physical shortcomings and desires. But what if that is not the case? What if our personality remains much the same after death, except without a body. What if our spirits retain their human traits and continue to make decisions and have desires much as we did in life. If this is indeed the case, then perhaps the murdered person will not automatically let go of the resentment felt towards his or her killer or killers. Such a powerful attachment to a single physical incident might then force the spirit to reincarnate with not only the physical results of the incident, but also the memories and, above all, a deep and lasting resentment towards the murderers. In a sense, the mind refuses to let go of the physical animosity, thereby barring itself from moving ahead spiritually and is reborn with all the significant traits of this animosity. So, we find, spirit acts in accordance with free will, and Karma acts in accordance to Karma. This may sound harsh, but we must remember that if we are to believe that the human soul is something more than our temporal personality we should consider that the purpose of life might be to gain experience of the physical in order to develop the spiritual. Life is important, but life as we know it is far from everything.

On the other hand, I would not want to take this argument too far, as one might conclude that every child born with a physical or mental defect was to blame for their own situation. There are a number of reasons why children are born with defects that can be linked to pharmaceuticals, drug abuse, under-nourishment, trauma and other ordinary, physical explanations. Perhaps their spirits chose these bodies for their own purpose, or perhaps once the soul enters the physical world, it has to abide by the nature of the physical until it departs, or perhaps none of the above. Clearly, all of this is speculation and, even if it makes some empirical sense, the meaning and mechanisms of the spirit are the theme of the last two chapters.

SUMMARY

Reincarnation is one of the dominant beliefs or theories as to what happens to the spirit when we die, but is generally rejected by western religion, philosophy and most of all science. Still, there exist a number of cases to date of reincarnation that are difficult to explain in any non-esoteric way. Explaining birthmarks and defects that correspond to the claimed previous personality, along with behavioural traits and a strong personal identification in young children, seems close to impossible using traditional means. Non-local consciousness as we have come to know it, however, has no difficulty in explaining and even supporting the notion of reincarnation. The only other alternative to reincarnation would be a variation of the super-psi theory, proposed in the previous chapter. Though this is a possible explanation, it fails to explain why only one child or current personality identifies itself with the previous personality, and why, if the process is truly non-local, the previous personality is so often in relatively close proximity in time and space. With this taken into the equation, the case for reincarnation seems indeed to provide reasonably sound evidence beyond any reasonable doubt of the postmortem survival of individual consciousness. Of our soul's survival beyond death, as it were.

With that statement I now conclude the evidential part of this book, and move on to a discussion into the nature of consciousness and some speculation into the meaning of life.

IX

CONCLUDING CONSCIOUSNESS

As we have seen, there is considerable evidence in favour of a non-local connection between mind and matter. Thousands of trials in laboratories all over the world have consistently demonstrated this, and though we cannot yet explain why this connection is there, it seems that the *Cartesian Cut* has been bridged. Or rather, it was never there. And if spirit or consciousness can influence not only inanimate material but also the physical bodies of others without any direct Newtonian connection, spirit should have little problem influencing its own designated body. Though many would, and do, argue that this is theoretically impossible, the practical evidence begs to differ. The spiritual and the material seem interwoven, not only in the mind of mystics, but in the world previously known as "material."

That spirit or consciousness has life-giving and life-sustaining properties seems clear from the evidence of healing. This lends further credibility to the notion that spirit infuses all things with life. The display of consciousness within single cells and plants, as explored by Cleve Backster among others, seems to corroborate this further.

The limitations of the mind, as indeed the very seat of consciousness, seem to be something quite different from that which modern science has led us to believe, as demonstrated by research into non-local consciousness. It seems almost as though our mind, as perceived through our brain, is a mere focal point of consciousness, rather than the seat and origin of the phenomenon. The non-locality demonstrated in modern mind research implies that consciousness, even our individual one, exists everywhere and independently of the constraints of time. This alone hints that consciousness is eternal whereas the body is temporal and destined to exist for a period of linear time only. In light of this it seems strange that our consciousness and sense of individuality should disperse merely because our brain ceases to function.

Neither does such a dispersal seem to be the case as we examine the near-death experience, where both perception and the sense of individuality are retained despite the fact that the brain, at least in a few spectacular cases, appears inanimate or "dead" by every modern medical standard. Yet in the near-death experience our consciousness seems to be able to operate not only as well as it does while the brain is active, but far better, allowing such features as panoramic vision, heightened sensory abilities and exceptional clarity of thought. In fact, physical restrictions, such as blindness or deafness, seem not to influence the sensory capacity of consciousness when liberated from its material host. Of the rival interpretations of Benjamin Libet's findings, the half second lapse before conscious awareness sets in described in Chapter 2, the notion that our temporal consciousness is ultimately controlled by something of a higher order stands out as the more likely alternative. Perhaps we are indeed directed by a "higher self" which reveals itself more freely and directly in situations such as the near-death experience, where the brain is not, or so it appears, the active interpreter of consciousness at all.

The physical evidence of reincarnation further implies that our consciousness retains a strong sense of individuality even for years[1] without a brain or body. This strong sense of individuality is sometimes so powerful that it appears to break through into the new body that consciousness inhabits, leaving both physical and mental signs.

Taken together, I find that this evidence makes a convincing case for postmortem survival of consciousness and the soul well beyond a "reasonable doubt." The only rival alternative, as scientific reductionism appears unable to explain the bulk of empirical evidence satisfactorily, is the super-psi hypothesis, which seems the less likely alternative. To make a bold yet, I feel, justifiable statement: all the evidence points towards the soul. So what, if anything, does this tell us about the soul?

What is Consciousness (Part II)

Our consciousness remains the link to our soul, but clearly the nature of this consciousness needs to be reassessed. To look upon consciousness merely as the complicated firing of neurones is not only rather depressing but is also, it would seem, unscientific. We must therefore look at consciousness in a completely new way, as indeed we must regard the entire physical universe. Such aspects as linear time and spatial distance seem to be, at least in part, creations of the brain, and the mind-over-matter aspect appears to defy the basic laws of Newton.

I would like to tentatively propose the following: *consciousness, and not the energy we recognise as matter, is the fundamental force that creates and sustains the universe.* This conclusion rests on the simple fact that mind can influence matter. If consciousness were indeed an illusion—a mirage created by the physical world—it should not be able to influence the physical world. The fact that consciousness has non-local qualities which the physical world lacks further suggests that it is more encompassing than the physical universe. Where the physical universe exists here and now, at least in a sense, the non-local universe exists everywhere and at all times. This leads me to the conclusion that the opposite is true: that non-local consciousness exists outside of and thus prior to the physical world, and that mind creates matter rather than that matter creates mind.

Actually, this is an oversimplification. It would be more correct, or so I believe, to state that *matter is an aspect of consciousness.* As mind and matter are obviously linked, they must have some basic and underlying common denominator or unifying principle. I believe that principle is to be found within the realm of non-local consciousness.

This notion is not new, I should add, and has been argued before by many mystics, philosophers and scientists. The philosopher Spinoza, a provocative freethinker active in the 16th century, is one such example. He felt that Descartes' *res cogitans* and *res extensa* were merely two aspects of the same underlying reality. This reality had infinite aspects, but the human mind was only capable of recognizing these two. Spinoza, interestingly enough, preferred using the term *consciousness* to the, at the time, far more popular *soul.* Though it took over a century for his fellow philosophers to dare to discuss his ideas openly, owing to their controversial nature, many of his notions can be found echoed in the theories of quantum physics. Here the world of consciousness and matter seem to come together, without the restraints of time and space and sometimes seemingly without causality—or at least without any cause and effect relationship that we have been able to pinpoint. If God plays dice or not still seems impossible to say.

Though many hopeful new-agers claim that the quantum world heralds the ultimate proof of the spiritual, this is not a view argued by physicists in general. The claim they are prone to make, when they make claims in this area at all, is usually that quantum physics does not disprove the spirit in the manner classical that physics does. There is, of course, quite a leap between *not disproving* and actually *proving* something.

Fortunately we need not move half-blinded by Heisenberg's *Uncertainty Principle* in the world of the minuscule to find evidence of Spinoza's mystical world. As we have seen, laboratories, experiments and researchers all over the world are churning out ample evidence on a level that even laymen can relate to. And relate to it we should, because if consciousness is the fundamental and eternal property of reality that it seems to be, then what we do with our individual minds is of quite profound importance. In fact, I would propose that we, through our own consciousness, set the parameters of our experience, not only in this life, but well beyond death.

An Eternity of Consciousness

What if our consciousness is eternal? What would that imply? Consciousness in the shape we experience as humans in the *here* and *now* deals with reality in specific ways. These ways were brought to our notice by the philosopher Immanuel Kant and defining them has since become one of the main objectives of psychology, of cognitive psychology in particular. Though it may be true that our minds can shape reality to some extent, we should remember that, as all relationships go, this is a two-way affair. Physical reality also shapes our consciousness, or rather we shape our minds in relation to physical reality (the brain itself being part of physical reality).

As we embark upon the development of consciousness in the guise of individual humans, we learn the rules of the physical world as this world is perceived by humans. Through this interaction we learn to define ourselves, both as mental and physical beings. In many cases we hold both to be the same, interchanging body with self. In other words, we look upon our bodies as our selves, as opposed to the temporal vessel of self that allows our consciousness to experience the physical world. This is a very practical trade-off as it allows us to operate as inhabitants of the physical world. Unfortunately, this also causes us no end of problems, from worrying about our physical appearance to the trauma of our eventual bodily demise (and possible loss of existence). Hopefully this book will help some people deal with the latter, but as long as we are here, the greater part of our consciousness is more intent on dealing with the physical than with questions of the hereafter.

Imagine then, if you will, waking up one morning and not having a body to confine *or define* you. In other words, imagine yourself as pure consciousness. What would be the parameters of your world and your self then?

What Then?

As I see it, it comes down to this: without a body we are simply mind. And though this mind is probably capable of understanding and actions well beyond what it is capable of while locked inside the body, this mind is heavily influenced by its sojourn within the physical. In other words, the kind of mind we develop during our life will influence the kind of consciousness we find ourselves with when that life ends. Both NDEs and reports of reincarnation seem to support this notion. That our consciousness is heavily influenced by the physical world is of particular importance as whatever our mind is set on during life there is always the physical to which we must relate. While alive and in human form the physical world is there for anyone to touch and deal with. But when we leave our physical body, reality will be what our consciousness chooses to perceive, as there will no longer be any physical parameters. No physical objects to bump into, if you will, and thus be forced to deal with. In other words, there is nothing at all to stop us from perceiving what we want to perceive, and only what we want to perceive. Our consciousness will be given full freedom to roam, much as it appears to do while we are dreaming.

This does not mean that the world of consciousness, or spirits if you prefer, is a random world without laws and parameters. But it is probably a world where it is even easier to become deluded and get lost than the physical one, consisting as it does of "pure" consciousness. Though all spirits may strive towards enlightenment, there is, after all, no reason why this should happen automatically at the moment of death. Consciousness, with all its implications, develops gradually through life and, to the best of my knowledge, there is no evidence suggesting that our consciousness should take one great leap into a state of perfection just because our physical body can no longer accommodate it. Death seems to me no more than a transition from one form of consciousness to another, with the essence remaining the same.

The point I am trying to make is that our minds are paramount. It is what we do with our minds, how open we are to new ideas, how we experience and control our own emotions, how we relate to others and ourselves, our inner discipline and all other expressions of who we let ourselves become, that is of importance. This is what we will have to deal with as we go beyond death, because it is the sum of this that will constitute "us", in a very real way. The problems and issues, hang-ups and obsessions that we develop and cultivate during life are not likely to disappear miraculously upon death, because they are part of who we are.

In short, what we do not deal with during life, we will have to deal with after life.

MINDSET

So am I saying that there is no divine entity, in one guise or another, waiting for us on the other side, as most religious faiths assume? Well, I see no reason why God or some aspect of such an inconceivable entity should not be waiting on the other side, much as I see no reason why God should not be present on this side. As the mystics claim, the Source is also the Destination, present along and in every step of the way. All I am suggesting is that our work is not over just because our life is over, just because we happen to die. Our consciousness sustains itself, and so we remain in essence who we are. What I doubt is merely that we should be condemned to an eternal heaven or hell, to reincarnate as slugs or saints, by an all-seeing and judgmental power, based solely on our performance during our physical life. Instead, I would propose that life and subsequent death with its release of consciousness is merely part of an ongoing process: the development of consciousness, or spirit, within and without the body.

Many organised religions promise their followers salvation and perfection upon death, provided they live their life in the right way. Unfortunately "the right way" has been contaminated as churches and similar organisations are inevitably human institutions, and as such are susceptible to every aspect of human nature, including the less inspiring traits that humans sometimes choose to include in their nature.

Human organisations often fill important purposes and are of great benefit to our societies, but it is nevertheless important to remember that whether religious or secular, they remain *human* organisations. It is always easy to get lost in a hierarchy, to lose one's grasp of the spiritual purpose behind the respective organisation, to mistake the flourishing of the organisation for the flourishing of the individual member of the congregation. Hierarchy in particular tends to give us the impression that some humans are closer to God than others. No doubt some minds are more developed than others, more in tune with their own selves, but I wouldn't equate this with being closer to God. Perhaps they have a finer intuition concerning the divine, being more harmonised with that which is divine in themselves, but that is about it. Unfortunately, there is no guarantee that positions in organised religions reflect such personal development. Yet we turn to pontiffs, clergy, evangelists, gurus and other supposedly enlightened figures when we seek our faith. Perhaps this is due to a sense of inferiority, that we feel it would be presumptuous to assume that we could answer our own spiritual questions, nurture our own souls. Perhaps there is comfort to be found in the rules and rituals of the *res extensa*, the outside world, that define who we are. *If we only obey the rules*, it is claimed, *salvation shall be ours*. Unfortunately, obeying rules is not always the best way to develop one's own consciousness; to the contrary, it is usually the opposite.

So we humans have historically tended to seek our interpretations of our "selves" and of our gods through others. Perhaps this is simply an expression of our need to belong, to define ourselves as part of a group or a tribe. Perhaps we want to believe that some people are closer to our god than we are because this means we won't have to shoulder the responsibility that comes with such a position. In any case, as the personal experience of the divine has taken a back seat to a more collective, second-hand version, so has the way by which we relate to the divine, the eternal, the spiritual. Instead of searching out the truth within ourselves, as is the mystical tradition, we have placed this responsibility in the hands of others.

The result ranges from the mild alienation of a weak personal faith to the irreversible mindset of blind dogmatism. None of these views are likely to be of much benefit to our consciousness as we pass beyond death. Nor are we likely to develop our minds and souls in the way we could, were we more active, and flexible, in searching out our own truths.

If our consciousness is an eternal force that we are ultimately in charge of, then sooner or later we will have to deal with whatever we make of our minds. What we make of life, we will also make of death.

I would propose that, as far as consciousness goes, like attracts like. If we are full of hate and resentment, then when we die our mind will probably seek out others and create a hellish environment until we come to terms with these feelings and turn away from them. If we have a strong belief in a particular kind of heaven, we will interpret what our consciousness perceives as that particular environment until we learn to see the bigger picture of who we truly are. If we expect simply to go to sleep while we wait for the horn of judgement day to blow, then we have set ourselves up for a pretty boring start to eternity. If we are convinced atheists, we might not even realise that we have died at all, hanging around the physical world in a state of confusion, much as in a dream or a nightmare. Certainly, we might believe that our consciousness is an illusion that will evaporate like smoke after death, as most reductionists do, but if consciousness is a real "thing", it will not simply disappear. Our mindset, along with its preconceived perceptions and obsessions, will remain.

ULTIMATE REALITY

I am not implying that the world of consciousness is an illusion of a different order, or that we continue to exist with our minds in universes of our own creation when we die, but I would argue that we exist in a universe of our own *interpretation*. In a reality of pure consciousness we must relate to everything through the nature of our own consciousness. If we are open-minded and know ourselves, what we perceive will undoubtedly be closer to the truth than if we have little knowledge of who we are and a lot of preconceived opinions as to what the afterlife, or this life for that matter, ought to be like.

Much of the evidence, albeit anecdotal, seems to support the notion that we go on to exist in a realm that mimics our pre-conceived opinions in some way. The stories describing the spiritual aspects of near-death experiences follow similar paths, but all contain subtle differences. It seems that often these differences are linked to the individual's faith or mindset. Where the Christian experiences the being of light as Jesus or as an angel, the agnostic often experiences a figure of great warmth and compassion, and some even claim that the figure of light is a confrontation with one's higher self. Who is to say which interpretation is the correct one? Perhaps all interpretations are correct, as consciousness itself seems to be linked to all things, past and present, material and immaterial.

It is also notable that most people who were firm and uncompromising in their beliefs before their NDE, apparently find themselves less rigid and dogmatic after the experience. The experience not only reduces the fear of dying, but apparently also tends to open the mind.[2] Perhaps this seems contradictory—that our consciousness should become more open if the experience is so completely dependent on a person's mindset—but as far as I can tell, these stories come from *mildly* dogmatic people, not *wildly* dogmatic ones. And the emphasis remains that an open mind is the best policy.

The less frequently occurring nightmarish near-death experiences also seem to confirm that mindset is an important factor. Those returning with tales of horror often seem to have a lot of unresolved anger and hostility, which the experience forces them to deal with. Had they not returned, perhaps they would have been stuck in their own personal hells for a while. A deeper study into the psychological makeup of those having such experiences would probably reward us with many new insights into the nature of human consciousness.

Other experiences describe travels in the realm between Earth and the spiritual, where confused souls roam the streets trying to get the attention of the living, hanging around bars trying to perpetuate addictions they had in life, and generally being unable to leave their earthly existence behind, or even to accept that they have died. These examples all seem to support the notion that consciousness locked into a particular mindset or belief-system will result in consequences beyond death.

The theme that consciousness during life is vitally important to what happens to us after life ends is by no means a new one. The famous psychic, Edgar Cayce, (who has been accredited with the ability to diagnose and successfully treat thousands of people given only their names while in a trance-like state), also reported a world between ours and the spiritual populated by disembodied souls unable to break free of their physical habits. Robert Monroe, the pioneer of the controlled out-of-body experience through the method of hemisphere-synchronisation, described a number of encounters with disembodied spirits on various intermediate levels between the *here* and *there*. The people reporting such experiences number in the thousands, and considering what we now know about consciousness, it would be foolish to discard these tales as "figments of the imagination." Indeed, one wonders if there are such things as figments of the imagination at all, given the non-local, reality-shaping nature of consciousness.

The tales of reincarnation suggest a similar importance to mindset. Though I believe reincarnation generally to be an orderly and well-planned process, I feel that in many of the cases featuring prominent birthmarks and birth defects reported by Stevenson the usual process might be bypassed by the firm intent of the mind. Instead of moving ahead into the world of consciousness after physical death, these reincarnation-oriented minds often seem too preoccupied with how the previous life has ended to be able to let go. In most cases, reincarnation is a natural part of their mindset, so the fact that they do reincarnate should come as no surprise. But by returning almost immediately to a new life, it seems as though their consciousness never worked through the issues of the past life. When born again, they retain much of the personality, not to mention animosity, of the previous life, as well as memories and physical traits. Those able to tell of their inter-mediate existence as spirits, and Stevenson reports several such cases, speak of hanging around the Earth-plane until they follow someone home, and attach themselves to a new life in the womb. Here again we find a powerful testament to the fundamental importance of mindset beyond death.

DREAMS AND DREAMERS

So what might a world of consciousness be like? Near-death experiences generally speak of something more real than reality itself, and I have no problem accepting this. As pointed out in Chapter 2, Consciousness, we humans perceive reality through our rather limited and limiting senses, so as pure consciousness we should be able to perceive reality in a much more pure, undis-torted way. As to what this would be like, I can only speculate.

Perhaps it is like a dream, yet a dream in which we remain not only lucid, not only aware of our selves, but "aware" on a com-pletely different level. Some people experience fragments of what this may be like in the so-called *hypnagogic* state prior to falling asleep, or sometimes in the process of waking up. In these in-stances it sometimes seems that we understand things with a clar-ity and complexity which the waking mind cannot even approach, but as we gradually awaken or *come to our senses*, it is almost as if the mind narrows and closes in on itself. Thoughts and whole concepts, which seemed profound only moments before, become abstract and elusive like smoke. Though these experiences, when I've had them, are unlike the usual cacophony of my dreams, I never used to take them seriously, preferring to explain them as illusions, as "mere" dreams. Now I find that perhaps this is not the case after all.

Acclaimed writer and physicist Fred Allan Wolf in his book *The Dreaming Universe* explores the idea that as we dream our minds are in communication with the mind of the universe. Dreaming, he claims, is not only necessary for the development of conscious-ness, but for the very sense of "self." This, too, makes more sense seen against the backdrop of non-local consciousness.

The notion that our mind reaches outside our body during dreaming is a popular one, with many proponents throughout history. The earliest parapsychological experiments in telepathy were actually undertaken by sleeping subjects,[3] and the significance of dreams is stressed in folklore as well as in a number of modern publications on the topic. Hemisphere synchronisation methods—using sound to balance the activity in both brain-halves, developed by the Monroe Institute[4] to induce out-of-body experiences—demonstrate distinctive brainwave patterns similar to those of people in deep meditation. Lucid dreaming[5] is another popular method of inducing out-of-body experiences and non-ordinary states of mind. Dreaming and meditation both seem to be more fundamentally connected to consciousness and physical reality than western science has previously presumed.

The ability to control our own mind, the power to induce non-ordinary states of awareness, often deeply spiritual, does seem to be available to us humans. Herein lies another significant aspect into the nature of consciousness; not only is it important to keep one's consciousness open and flexible, it is also important to train and develop one's consciousness. After all, apart from it being the only thing we can bring with us beyond death, it is our sole means of existence and orientation once we let go of the body.

HUMAN CONSCIOUSNESS REVISITED

So far I have used the terms consciousness, mind, soul and spirit interchangeably. The purpose has been to point to the same underlying qualities, or the basic "sameness" of these concepts. However, the term "consciousness" in particular is confusing, as it seems to take on different forms in different situations, while the others remain more constant in their respective denotations. For instance, consciousness while awake is different from consciousness during sleep, which in turn is different from non-local consciousness, which again is different from the kind of consciousness that is active during a near-death experience. So what is consciousness?

I would propose that consciousness is that which facilitates awareness. In different situations, this awareness will manifest itself in different ways. Thus, consciousness is not the same as spirit or soul, but rather the process by which the spirit or soul creates or retains awareness. This includes awareness of both self and surroundings. This would imply that "we," as we experience ourselves, are not our souls, but rather interpretations of them. Human consciousness allows us only a fraction of the awareness which pure "soul" consciousness would allow. Beyond death we will, hopefully, become one again with this more encompassing nature—our "greater self"—but from the vantage point of human perception, we can only experience part of what we truly are. Indeed, it seems quite possible that our souls, when no longer bound to a human body, can only experience as much of reality as they have learned to cope with, however much "greater" the world of spirit might seem as compared to the world of body.

I would argue that it is this greater self, our soul, which attempts to direct our bodies through our thoughts and actions, allowing our human self to be the focal point of our experience. The split-second lapse of consciousness detected by Benjamin Libet would thus represent our brain's interpretations of our soul's actions, human consciousness translating that which is barely comprehensible into terms humanly understandable. This does not mean that as humans we are mere puppets acting out the will of our soul, as we ultimately *are* our souls, but it means that the seat of our consciousness may well be elsewhere than inside our craniums.

Human "local" consciousness may indeed be capable of a more pure or more direct connection to spirit through meditation, hypnosis, dreaming or some other method of integrating non-local consciousness. Indeed, those people we hold as most spiritually advanced seem to be in near to complete control of their physical nature rather than the other way around, unlike the rest of us. Perhaps we need only apply our minds to lessen the interference of our brains to do this. This would certainly seem to be the basic instruction for successful meditation: the calming of mind.

The notion that our soul is different—in a sense separate—from our human self may sound strange and confusing, but that is mainly due to the fact that we, as humans, reason in terms of causality and locality in space and time. Understanding our surroundings in terms of separateness—of causality along the one-way path linear time and local space—is a construction of the human brain, a property of human consciousness if you will. Reality itself, as demonstrated by both physicists on the quantum level and researchers dealing with non-local consciousness, is not necessarily confined to laws of space-time and paradigms of separateness. On the contrary, everything appears to be connected, paying little heed to such constraints as time or space.

As demonstrated in remote viewing, our mind can reach out anywhere in time and space. Experiments in precognition defy causality, and some experiments even successfully combine psychokinetics with *postcognition*, or influencing the past through conscious intent in the present.[6] That we in human form should thus be separated from our souls is merely an illusion made possible by the use of human local consciousness. Again we are reminded of the limitations of consciousness in human form. The purpose and necessity of such a limitation, however, is the topic of the next chapter.

Consciousness deals with information, and information has a unique property: it is used to understand and shape the physical, yet it is not physical in itself. Information is also something we can give away yet still keep, and unlike anything else in the physical, it is unlimited. There always seems to be room for more. In a sense, information is a symbolic representation of the spiritual. It is full of meaning, yet exists nowhere in space. The ink on this paper exists and so does the shape of the words, but where do they become meaningful information? "In the brain" is an obviously inadequate answer as we live in a universe of non-local proportions (especially given the fact that *non-local proportions* is a contradiction in terms). So it might be beneficial to look upon spirit in terms of information: limitless and full of meaning, but said meaning depending on what we chose to store and actively use.

IMPLICATIONS OF CONSCIOUSNESS

The implications of the research presented in this book not only concern the afterlife, but also demand that we seriously reconsider practically every aspect of life as we know it. Our individual minds would seem to be, to a varying degree, in constant communication with everything that surrounds us, other minds in particular. More importantly, our individual minds are able to shape reality in subtle ways.

It should be remembered that reality can be ultimately regarded as a process as demonstrated by quantum physics, rather than as a "thing." That which we regard as an *object* is actually the representation of quantum mechanical *processes* as interpreted by our mind. The world that we perceive is closer to the concept of an *action* than the concept of a *thing*. And actions are far easier to influence with the mind than things.

So we find that our state of mind will not only influence the way we feel and the way our body functions, but also influences other people and the behaviour of the world in general. The overall implication of *field consciousness*, for instance, is that we would do well to create a society where peoples' minds thrive; other problems would then sort themselves out. I think it is a fair assessment of modern society to say that we cater mainly to bodily needs and the shallowest aspects of the mind. In a society where minds are dominated by frustration, resentment, animosity and other less constructive qualities, it is possible and even likely that physical aspects will be affected. Not to mention the effect these single minds will have upon each other or the mass-mind on the individual.

Psychologists talk of an effect known as *group think* in which a group of people begin reasoning in a particular direction, gaining momentum and usually ending at a bad decision as the capacity to think critically becomes gradually more impaired. Everyone just goes with the flow towards a single destination. It is not hard to imagine psi at work here or at a more global level. Few individuals in influential positions in society seem to act rationally from a humanitarian perspective, a state of affairs that is often ascribed to faults in political and socio-economical systems, but perhaps an underlying factor is also the field consciousness of a disgruntled humanity. The problems "in our mind" may well spill out into the physical world and the minds of others. This is important to consider in our dealings with others, for our own sake and for theirs. Negative thought against others may influence them, and we should take care to shield ourselves against the negative thoughts of others. None of this, of course, means that we deserve everything that happens to us, but it implies that we are far more than helpless pawns in the game of life.

The applied use of our emerging understanding of consciousness could boost many disciplines into new areas that should prove highly beneficial to the individual. If prayer or other forms of more direct healing prove as successful as preliminary research show, healthcare could be revolutionised. Many people would recover faster and with fewer complications and less medication. Indeed, perhaps many would not require invasive treatment such as surgery in the first place.

If education would focus on consciousness itself, rather than cluttering it with junk it has no real use for, as often is the case, this too would create a revolution with consequences almost impossible to foresee. Imagine a world where schoolchildren learn meditation, creative visualisation, remote viewing and other mental skills on a daily basis. Would they grow up to be adults prone towards war and other such drastic answers to conflicts? Would they even recognise "conflict" in the sense we do, being trained to recognize what unifies rather than what divides? As most people who take part in such experiments, constituting pretty much a cross-section of society, find these to have deep personal and spiritual significance, a different future altogether would seem to be the likely outcome.

This emerging understanding into the nature of consciousness probably provides the greatest affront to psychology, but also promises the greatest benefits. Few self-respecting psychoanalysts are likely to feel comfortable with the notion that a person's problems lie not in such local factors as her early youth, but might instead originate in a previous life, which becomes a possibility if reincarnation is to be accepted. On the other hand, hypnotherapy may prove useful to get in touch with one's "true" consciousness where other therapeutic counselling has failed.[7] In any case, the art of mind-healing will need to accommodate the reality of non-local consciousness along with its implications if it is going to thrive in the future.

The phenomenon of precognition is likely to turn much of business on its head, dealing as it does with appraising the future. As researchers have been successful in predicting the rise and fall of the Wall Street Stock Market using remote viewing into the future,[8] it is likely that this practice will become widespread. The consequences of such a feedback loop backward through causality are hard to imagine, but it is likely that both stock markets and other forms of gambling would eventually have to close down.

The focus on the mental and spiritual, rather than on the material, will hopefully also make its imprint on the market, focussed as it currently is on selling us material things to make us feel better about ourselves. As we become aware that "feeling better" in this life is mainly a question of consciousness, we are likely to take a greater interest in those products and activities that help us more directly with this central issue, rather than with those dealing mainly with alleviating symptoms. The fastest car, the best paying job, and the latest designer clothes might not offer the same allure in the future as they do now. More time devoted to contemplation, new experiences and stimulating conversation with friends, helping others and developing one's own consciousness might well become far more tempting options.

In the future, police, fire-fighters and other rescue personnel may use "psychics" on a regular basis, or actively train to develop their own intuition. Where psychics in the past would scan buildings for ghosts or poltergeists, their modern counterparts might "sense" faulty electrical wiring or possible future gas leaks. Imagination and talent would seem to be the only limits as to what potential disasters could be sensed and avoided in this way.

Remote viewing has demonstrated that the era of secrets may be coming to an end. In a world where secretiveness seems so emphasised—by governments to maintain the security of the state and by commercial organisations to keep their competitive edge—the reality of remote viewing is bound to come as a shock. One wonders what it would be like to live in such a world, where nothing can remain a secret.

It is indeed hard to imagine any aspect of society that would not, in the long run, be fundamentally changed by what we seem to be able to do with consciousness. True, at present the effects are slight, from the gentle nudging of random number generators and of subconscious responses in our autonomic nervous systems, to the often partially correct remote viewing sessions, but this is only the beginning. When electricity was first discovered, it was used by scientists to cause twitching in severed frogs legs; today it is used to power every city on Earth and almost everything else. In a similar vein, that the effects of psi are generally very slight at present does not mean they cannot become powerful tools for humanity in the future. We might also expect that to wield these tools, a certain level of maturity in the individual mind will be required. Given the spiritual aspects of the psi experience, there is, I believe, good reason to harbour some hope on this account. It is hard to imagine anyone developing his or her non-local consciousness to any great degree, yet retaining narrow-mindedness and other less beneficial aspects of ordinary human consciousness.

Why Human Consciousness

Why Human Consciousness at all, one might wonder? Certainly a different kind of consciousness seems to exist, non-local and unencumbered by the physical constraints of space and time, so why bother with cramming this virtually limitless consciousness into the confines of the human brain? The answer, obviously, is because human consciousness, which deals with the world in a local and causal way, serves a purpose. Perhaps it would be more correct to say that being *a human* serves a purpose for consciousness. What that purpose might be is the purely speculative topic of the final chapter, but a few points are appropriate to make here.

Consciousness in a human seems to have far more options and a wider range of available actions than the other alternatives (e.g., consciousness expressed by an animal or a plant) available on Earth. Development of consciousness, which I assume to be one of the fundamental desires, purposes and goals of mind, is simply better facilitated by the human form. Sure, perhaps it would be interesting to experience a few hundred years as a tree, but what is there to make of that experience? As a tree, our consciousness might experience pain and pleasure of a sort as well as a different bond with the Earth, yet it would probably not know how to deal with this sensation beyond merely acknowledging it. (Of course, at the cellular level our consciousness probably experiences the world much as the plant does anyway.) As humans we can simply experience a wider range of experiences than we would were our consciousness of a less complex form. Perhaps the variation as well as the options based upon this is the name of the game.

So why limit consciousness at all? This is another good question, and one brilliantly addressed by Aldous Huxley in his book, *Doors of Perception*. The book basically revolves around the author's mescaline experience, and raises many questions about the nature of both reality and religion. Huxley argued that the brain does not construct reality as much as it filters it. Reality experienced unfiltered is a mystical, unifying and deeply fulfilling experience, and it is the brain's purpose to narrow the experience down in order for us to be able to function as human individuals. In the subjectively fulfilling state of bliss and all-knowing that Huxley experienced, human affairs become quite pointless, as indeed does human existence. To function as a human being, it is necessary for the brain to "shield" the mind from the true nature of things, as reality itself is far too mystical and fulfilling if revealed as itself. While on certain drugs, the mind does not "hallucinate" as much as "opens up," according to Huxley.

I am prone to agree, at least in part, with these conclusions. I believe that the world as seen through the mind rather than the brain would reveal reality to be a different and more meaningful experience than we are used to. Many near-death experiences support this, as does deep meditation. And though I do not have an ethical problem with people using drugs to experience mystical states, I feel there are some practical issues that should be taken into consideration. Mainly, the mind/brain under the influence of drugs is not as easy to control consciously as through non-drug methods.[9] Also, the use of drugs has a quick-fix quality, a mentality that can be addictive in itself, for which there is ample evidence in our society. Though drug-induced experiences can be both interesting and perhaps even profoundly meaningful to many people, what we want to experience we would do well to learn to experience through our minds alone. Drugs are a physical thing, they influence the brain in physical ways, yet consciousness would appear to be far more than merely a physical phenomena. Ultimately, when we have no brain or physical body to rely on, we can only expand our consciousness by consciousness itself. Our minds are, in the end, who we are.

Explaining why human consciousness is not different from what it is does not, of course, answer why it takes the form it actually does. So let us postulate that human consciousness has the limitations and parameters it has, because it poses the right kind of challenge. Obstacles demand that we use our minds and, in the process, develop our consciousness to get past them, and human life is full of such obstacles. The human brain and its particular form of perception is, in itself, an obstacle for consciousness at a higher level. In short, one might argue that being human is a challenge for the soul, a challenge necessary for the soul to develop.

New Realms

A good theory does not invent extra realms, "other worlds" or new forces or energies without very good reason and without providing independent evidence that they exist.[10] These words, expressed by Susan Blackmore, are simple, crucial and to the point, and deserve to be addressed.

Clearly we are suggesting such "extra realms," so the question is: do we have a very good reason and can we provide independent evidence that they exist? The answer, as far as my consciousness is capable of deducing, is *yes*. All the evidence offered in the previous chapters is, though culturally controversial, *reliable* and, when possible, *repeatable*. Most critics have abandoned the design-flaw argument, as test designs become more rigorous without affecting results. The "coincidence" argument seems much like clutching at straws, as it would require coincidences of astronomical proportions. Coincidence also becomes less likely with each trial added to the case load, which furthers the gap between this alternative and the empirically speaking, less far-fetched, non-local properties of consciousness. After all, quantum physics has grappled with the non-locality issue since Max Planck initiated the quantum revolution a century ago, and modern scientific materialism has not objected to these findings. Why then should the notion that non-locality might be a part of reality on our level be such a provocative idea? After all, our level of reality, the physical world as we perceive it with our ordinary senses, inevitably builds on or consists of the quantum level.

The only other likely alternative explanation to the findings presented here is the superpsi theory, which requires new realms of at least the same complexity as would the soul. Actually, the soul may well turn out to have the qualities of superpsi, which would, in turn, make superpsi a part of the spiritual universe made of consciousness suggested here. But these are merely answers and interpretations, arising from the limits of my own consciousness as a human being, my own *mindset*, as it were. It is for you, dear reader, to review the evidence and draw your own conclusions as to the nature of consciousness and how this in turn might apply to your own life and mind.

For me, at least, it seems that as we leave this life to go beyond death, we can only bring that which we have made out of our consciousness. I hope that this book might help some minds make a bit more of that consciousness and so, perhaps, help with the transition, and in dealing with the beyond.

X

THE GREAT MYSTERY

As the reader will have noticed, this book has addressed the issue of spirit from the most practical standpoint available. This might have given a slightly clinical impression of spirit—which is unfortunate—but merely a side effect of the clinical nature of scientific protocol. I would like to stress that I do not believe that spirit can be measured, weighed and understood in any way other than the most superficial using the instruments of science. As I pointed out in the introduction, the purpose of this book was not to define spirit in any way, but merely to prove that spirit has its place in the natural order of things. The purpose of proving the soul's viability from the scientific standpoint is to motivate people to start taking this aspect of their lives far more seriously than they generally seem to be doing. To balance the scientific intent of the previous chapters, and to give to those of a more spiritual inclination something to ponder, I have dedicated this final chapter to a purely spiritual approach.

In this chapter I would like to present a few thoughts on what spirit is. These thoughts and views are subject to change (and may well be completely off target), so there is no need to accept them just because the previous chapters made sense. I hope the reader will cut me some slack in writing about this topic because words cannot really convey what the life of a spirit is all about. Also, I hope that those readers who are less amused with spiritual speculation and picked up this book based on its scientific stance will not judge me too harshly. I would understand such a reaction as this chapter is, indeed, a deviation from empirical science, but given what the empirical data has suggested so far, a bit of mystical speculation does not seem completely out of place. A book concerning the existence of the human soul would be a bit of a cop-out if it did not contain some philosophical speculation into the origin, purpose and destination of said soul.

Evidence supporting the human spirit may be no different from evidence supporting the force of gravity or the dynamics of evolution, but there is a teleological component to the former. Spirit exists for a reason—or so we presume—whereas gravity and evolution simply exist, are a part of the complex and dynamic laws of nature, but demand no deeper reason in order to play this part. Perhaps there is, indeed, a purpose to these laws of nature, a cause that predates such natural laws and the universe itself, but science has never required such a purpose to explain its take on reality. God or spirit is a hypothesis that is not required for this particular equation. The dynamics that spirit need comply with, on the other hand, should reasonably reside where spirit or consciousness resides, which is evidently well beyond the parameters of the laws of nature as we recognise them. To even begin to understand spirit, we must go beyond the physical world as our human consciousness perceives it. Naturally, this might be a put-off for the scientifically disposed reader, but nevertheless I hope he or she will read on. And bear in mind that the great mystery would not be such a great mystery if we could figure it out. This is, ironically perhaps, the great thing about mystery—without mystery we could not develop our minds in new ways.

The Nature and Purpose of Spirit

What better place to start than at the beginning? Spirits, I believe, are of an eternal nature, created by the Source, the Prime Mover, First Cause or God. The creative force I'm speculating about here is not to be equated with the dignified elderly gentleman beside the anthill described in the first chapter, or with any other human concept proposed by our various religions. The nature of this all-encompassing source of consciousness or Great Spirit is well beyond the capacity of human comprehension. To even begin to comprehend this force, we would have to develop our consciousness well beyond that of any human—which indeed might be the ultimate goal and purpose of spirit.

We, as individual souls, could be seen as sparks of the divine that are given free will and consciousness. As such, we are separate entities from this conscious and creative force, allowed to wield our free will through our consciousness in order to create and develop our individuality; yet we remain part of the eternal force that gave us life to begin with. And, as individual spirits, it lies in our nature to strive back towards the Source, towards our origin, which thus also becomes our destination. Along the path we learn, become more than we were, and finally, through returning to our point of origin, contribute to the whole and enrich the Source. It is only natural to suppose that such a path would take us through many lives and many forms of existence in many different worlds—not only on Earth—but always according to the wishes of our individual spirit, our true and eternal self.

From my point of view, a single life on Earth followed by a passing over to some blissful—or, in some cases, not so blissful—afterlife, appears to be a less likely alternative. Indeed, it makes little sense at all to me. Rather, it makes sense that our sojourn as a human be but one of many experiences that we should attempt to make the best of. Though it is not an experience to be taken lightly—because all and every life is important—neither is it something we should beat ourselves up too much about. If for no other reason than because life in the human form is probably one of the toughest learning opportunities the universe provides. After all, while in human form, there is nothing that our consciousness can know for sure, beyond the shadow of a doubt. There are no objective truths to serve as a beacon to strive against, to light our way. There are no subjective truths to serve as a compass, to guide us. Though many people "know" beyond any doubt that there is a right way and a wrong way, that there is a God, that we live forever, this knowledge remains opinion, for this is the nature of existence on Earth. Be the basis of one's belief the empirical process and whatever scientific paradigm this leads to, or the dogmatic interpretation of a religious document, belief remains belief. After all, even if the survival of our consciousness beyond death seems as likely and predictable as the behaviour of apples in a field of gravity, we cannot know for sure until we experience it firsthand. We can, as humans, simply not know anything beyond doubt. This is why we invented the term *reasonable doubt*, for reason can only take us this far. Faith exists in a domain of its own, and faith is ultimately what human convictions boil down to. The fact that there are no facts (yes, a contradiction, but truth, it is said, hides in contradictions and mystery) does not mean that our spirit is absent or passive as we stumble through our lives knowing nothing for sure, but all too often we get excessively caught up in the physical, seldom finding the calm needed to pay attention to our soul. Life as a human, as any human, is difficult, but it is also something that we chose as spirits with our own free will. The objective of this unsure, faith-demanding experience being to further our consciousness, and thus the human experience is something we should attempt to get through without violating what we believe in. After all, what we believe in might actually turn out to be true. Just because we can't know anything for sure does not mean that the truth isn't out there, as the saying goes.

The purpose of developing our fledgling consciousness is to become, in essence, the same as the Source—or so I believe. By arriving through our free will at the will and consciousness of the Source, we will be of a common "substance" (for lack of a better term) and, as such, indiscernible from the Source or Creator. In other words, our purpose is to become one with our Creator, which we can only achieve through our own effort by becoming the same in spirit as the creator. It might sound blasphemous to some that we should be able to become like God by ourselves, but then one must remember that we are of God to begin with, and are given this essence for that very purpose. This notion is one which mystics from practically every religious denomination endorse in one form or another, yet it is also a fairly simple and rational system—or so it seems to me. It makes sense, especially if consciousness is the fundamental "matter" of the universe, for what other challenge could mind have than to grow, develop, evolve and finally understand everything (itself) fully and completely?

Rational a belief or not, a number of objections can be made to the source and destiny of souls as proposed here, and I would like to address the more common ones. For one thing, one might argue, if the Source is perfect, why create less than perfect spirits that have to struggle a great deal merely to return to their origin? Though it may be both futile and foolish to use human logic to explain such metaphysical questions, few sceptics are likely to accept the limits of human consciousness as a valid argument. I sympathise with this notion; after all, to question things and to make sense of them is one of the purposes for occupying a body in the first place. One of the simplest and most eloquent, not to mention logically appealing, myths of creation is found among the native populations of North America, and it addresses some of these objections. In this version of creation, the Great Spirit exists in completeness and perfection. Being perfect means that there is no conflict, no strife, no tension and no challenges within the Great Spirit. This also means, in a sense at least, that there can be no development, as development demands some kind of challenge. To make further development possible, the Great Spirit created Mother Earth and sends tiny portions of itself down to her—little spirits in human form—that they may grow and return as larger spirits than the sparks they were when they left. The cynical sceptic might, and generally does, ask why the Great Spirit would want to grow at all if it is perfect to begin with. But most cynics, sceptical or not, will readily agree that the desire (for lack of better word) to grow can be found in everything on Earth from the bacteria to the flower to the multinational corporation; and why should the world of spirits—great or small—be any different? If matter takes on more complex forms over the ages, if life evolves into more complex forms, why should not consciousness strive to do so also? Indeed, perhaps this is why all things seem strive towards more complex forms in the first place, for this is what consciousness—that which all things consist of—does. And unlike the physical, the spiritual is without limitations, without a conceivable end. The physical world is limited to a number of atoms which bacteria, flowers and multinational organisations all must compete over in their different ways. This is not the case with the spiritual, where growth is an unlimited option available to all.

Still, why go through so much hardship as an individual, less-than-perfect spirit to attain perfection? Is there not a simpler way? Well, perhaps there exist easier alternatives than human life on Earth, but there are benefits to reaching destinations by more difficult paths. Take, for instance, the physical path towards the peak of a mountain. Those who climb are far more likely to enjoy both the view and who they have become through their struggle than the ones who were effortlessly transported in a helicopter and dropped off at the peak. A limited parable, as always, but adequate in that it demonstrates the connection between struggle and development. Change, whether of a physical, mental or spiritual nature, does not come about in some miraculous way all by itself; rather it demands an effort in proportion to the desired change. The steps we need to take to develop our selves cannot be taken for us. We need to fight our own battles, slay our own dragons, climb our own mountains; what we experience and learn will only be in proportion to that we invest in risk and effort. Perhaps this, too, is a natural law of spirit.

To sum up the incalculable: the purpose of spirit is to become one with the Source by becoming *as* the Source, but also to bring the added wealth of experience *into* the Source. The experiences of the parts brings wealth to the whole, which would not be possible if the whole were not of parts. Perhaps we, in our small, individual ways, help the source experience itself.

Understanding Spirit

Spirituality takes on proportions that are difficult to come to terms with from the human point of view, mired down as we are in the here-and-now of our subjective, local and temporal experience of the world. Some people equate their spirit with their human personalities whereas others, such as those who believe in reincarnation, may look upon their spirit as the accumulation of personalities. In either case, the nature of our soul as suggested here goes well beyond human, physical personality, both in terms of lives, of purpose and of consciousness. For if our spirit is our true nature, our personality is merely our temporal nature. Any understanding of spirit from the human point of view is bound to be subject to misconception through the contamination of our here-and-now personalities, something with which we must somehow come to terms. Still, as we can know nothing with absolute certainty, and as this limitation has not stopped humanity in any endeavour so far, there is no reason why it should not stop us in this spiritual inquiry either. Keeping in mind that anything claimed about spirit must remain speculative, and will never come closer to the truth than a fair and symbolical assessment.

So assuming that spirit is the eternal force within us, and as such it is infinitely more than our current human personality, it is also, to some degree, synonymous with us. Perhaps if we were to strip our personalities of all of our physical desires and needs, we might arrive at our spirit, or at least a portion of it. Yet, at the same time, spirit itself belongs in a domain well beyond the horizon or scope of human consciousness. A tricky issue to come to terms with, and perhaps another one of those contradictions where truth hides out. So, given our obvious limitations, what would be fair to assume about spirit and how it relates to the individual life?

In his book, *Journey of Souls*,[1] Dr. Michael Newton presents accounts of humans who, while under deep hypnosis, describe their experiences of an existence between physical lives—lives lived both on Earth and elsewhere. What makes these accounts particularly interesting is that the thousand or so subjects all describe this state of being in similar ways. As spirits between lives—or so people under deep hypnosis report—much effort is spent in analysing the behaviour of the previous life in order to learn from it, and preparation is made for the next. More advanced spirits apparently also learn to create portions of physical worlds, and other feats of applied consciousness. The order of the spiritual world would appear to be a striving towards more advanced states at one's own pace, applying one's own mind and free will along with other spirits belonging to the same "cluster." The more advanced spirits help the less advanced ones as a means of their own advancement, the emphasis being on learning and development throughout the spiritual. During each life as a human, we are supposed to experience certain things as well as test our own spiritual development and, after each life is completed, we return to the spiritual to work our way through the life we have just lived. Again this implies that what we do not deal with during this life, we must inevitably deal with later. The world of spirits is described by Dr. Newton's many subjects as one without secrets, animosity or hierarchy as we would recognise it. A world where learning and teaching is accomplished through love and compassion, and where time flows in a very different manner than it does on Earth. A pure and eternal state of being where the single human life—this experience that completely engulfs us in the here-and-now—is regarded more as an experience and opportunity and less as an identity. These findings are echoed to different degrees by other therapists such as Dr. Brian Weiss, Dr. Roger J. Woolger and Dr. Stanislav Grof, all of whom have written interesting books on the topic. Indeed, the notion that we lead a complex and fulfilling life while not occupying a human body is supported by many religious denominations and would seem to be growing in popularity across the board.

When pondering these accounts of spirits and how they relate to their different bodies and physical lives, I am reminded of the role-playing games I indulged in with my friends when I was a teenager. We would roll the dice and act out the parts of warriors and magicians, elves and trolls, spacemen, vampires and a host of other real or imaginary creatures conceivable by human imagination. We would relate to our "characters" as parts of ourselves, often feeling quite passionately about the more successful and favored ones. We gave them life of a sort and they, in turn, enriched our lives. Perhaps then our spirits regard their individual lives as humans with their respective personalities in a similar way. Where we saw role-playing as a game to enjoy and perhaps advance in, our spirits might see life as an opportunity to learn through the experience of being human. Though our human form fears death as "the end," our spirit knows that our consciousness will continue to exist, even after the final die has been cast and the once so lively character has succumbed to the rules of the game and can roam this particular world no more.

Virtual Reality of Souls

I would like to remain in the land of allegory for a while, as this seems as good a place as any to expand consciousness. Imagine if you will a not too distant future, where Virtual Reality simulators have been perfected to the level that they are indiscernible from actual reality. Imagine also that, when entering such a simulator, subjective time flows much faster than actual time, which allows the player to experience an imaginary world for a full lifetime though only five minutes of real-time actually passes. In other words, imagine being able to live an entirely different life in less time than it takes to drink a cup of coffee. Would you be tempted to enter such a game, to have such an experience? Of course, once in the game, there is no way to stop playing until the "death" of your character, or whatever you are embodying. Most people would probably feel some trepidation about doing this even if it were not "for real." And as these "reality games" need not restrict themselves to the parameters of human life, virtually any kind of existence could be experienced. Imagine, for instance, a game that allowed you to experience the life of a dolphin at sea, far from humans. Not only to feel the sea and become as one with your dolphin body, but taking it one step further and actually process information in the same way a dolphin does. How long would it take before your real life seemed a distant dream, and in how many "years" would it be forgotten altogether? And what if, for the duration of the game, you would not be allowed to recall your actual origin, the person you really are, because this might spoil the game. Would you still be willing to play it? Perhaps, if there were different games to chose from, some less taxing than an entire life on Earth. Perhaps if they were shorter in subjective time or simpler, or allowed the player to be in contact with "real" life at some level, people might be more prone to try one. Different games, different challenges, different rewards, but all of them providing new experiences and perspectives, enriching consciousness.

This is what souls do, only on a much grander scale—or so I believe. Some souls choose easier games or experiences for the same reasons we humans would. Others choose more challenging ones, because there is far more to learn this way; and life on Earth is probably one of the most challenging "games" souls get to experience. Challenging because of its demanding physicality (we need food, sleep, shelter and much more merely to survive), because nothing is certain and because we are cut off from our true selves and have no easy way to remember who we really are. As humans we should give ourselves an encouraging pat on the back because it seems that this is a pretty tough school. In fact, Newton's patients attest that many spirits—in particular the younger ones—report shock at how hostile humans can be, how little we seem to care about each other compared to the warm and compassionate existence in the spiritual. Many souls take quite a beating during life, or so it seems, and need time to recover in spirit. Many do not wish to return. On the other end of the scale, others get hooked on life, become addicted to it, and cannot wait to get back. Still others get so confused in human form that they get virtually lost upon death, due to physical addictions, dogmatic misconceptions, or just the inability to let go of their former physical life. Many such stories from several different sources—not only Newton's patients—convey the notion that human life is not easy.

So the Earth-experience would appear to be a tough school for spirits, but one that offers lessons not to be had anywhere else. Time—or rather, effort—spent on Earth is well invested from the spiritual perspective as the learning benefits are many. Yet we know, as spirits, that life is going to be tough and that when we return to our true home we will still be responsible for our actions along with the karma we will have accumulated along the way. These would seem to be the two points that the virtual reality allegory fails to take into consideration. Life is not a game in the human sense of the word, and we are ultimately held accountable for what we do—or at least we hold ourselves accountable for it.

RELATING TO SPIRIT

So now we have a few ideas about how our spirit might relate to being human, but how are we as humans to relate to something as incomprehensible as our spirit? After all, the more complex has an easier time comprehending the less complex than vice versa. The notion of being "merely" one of several lives is likely to raise such questions as "who am I", but on the other hand, are not such questions applicable to any single life? Are we really only one personality as humans or are we perhaps several, a constant dance of different qualities fighting for dominion? Perhaps we consider these different "personages" to be the same person merely because we share the same memories, the same points of reference and the same consciousness? Certainly, most of us behave in different ways with different people and express different traits in different situations, almost as if we had transformed into a different person ourselves. Yet, whatever sub-personality or character from our gallery we act out, we remain the same physical being, the same person. Maybe our spirit relates to each individual life and personality in the same way that we relate a single personality trait to the sum of our personality. When attempting to relate to spirit from the perspective of being a human, it is easy to get the feeling that one is merely a puppet, that our spirit is the puppeteer who jerks our strings and controls our every move half a second before "we" act—or believe we act—as Libet's experiments imply. This is a strange and not very empowering feeling to harbour, but a spirit seems such a vast, powerful thing when compared to the limited and temporal humans that we are. But then, we must also recognise that we are our spirit now, that we are indeed jerking our own strings, and experiencing our own thoughts and choices as a human. That we are spirits in human guise, and that our actions remain our own, in some strange and dimly understood feedback loop. Beyond death our minds will, hopefully, open themselves up to their full capacity and we will again be fully our spiritual selves, none the worse for wear, and a few steps further along our respective paths of development. This is a far more empowering thought.

Though I have argued that we are mainly a point of reference for a spirit existing outside space-time, I am convinced that our spirit is always with us, in whatever form our consciousness allows. Yet spirit, like non-local consciousness, is not confined to the limitations of space or time, which means that our spirit can be elsewhere as well as here with us at the same time. This is merely one more of those contradictions that the human brain is unable to grasp until we manage to think in terms other than linear time and space. For all we are able to comprehend, our spirit may be occupying more than one physical body at the same time, or may be active simultaneously at another level, in another dimension. Due to the restrictions of our human consciousness, we are only aware of the human level of this existence, which does not have to mean that "we" are anything less than our full spirit. When we die it will not necessarily feel like meeting "the rest of us," but may rather feel like expanding into our greater self. We remain, in essence, the same as we were, only infinitely more. In a sense this may be like waking up from a dream, only to find that life was the dream all along.

The idea of a greater self with a more advanced consciousness may be possible to come to terms with, but how this greater self might interact with, and even be influenced by, our human consciousness would seem to go well beyond anything conceivable to us. The idea can seem simple at first, but the more one contemplates it, the more complex it becomes, inevitably bordering on the contradictory. For example, while it may be hard to accept that a remote viewer can see things which have yet to take place, the implication that the future can somehow be accessed before it "happens" is almost impossible to comprehend. The apparent division between human self and spirit self is another such contradiction.

Popular Western religious and philosophical traditions may make these notions of post-mortem activity difficult to accept. After all, repeated reincarnation into a number of different dimensions, with intermediary schooling for souls, is not a familiar theme to Western thought. This tradition is generally focused on our going to a heaven of one shape or another where we are to live out our days for an eternity of blissful peace (unless we are unfortunate enough to end up somewhere less comfortable for a similar term). The idea that when we die we must continue to develop as souls—with life being merely one distance along a very long track—is going to be provocative to many people. The cognitive obstacle we need to overcome to deal with the issue is our taste for dichotomy. We, in Western thinking at least, tend to reason in terms of polarity, of excluding relationships. "You can't have your cake and eat it, too" as the saying goes. We think in terms of good or evil, life or death, heaven or hell—semantics that invariably shape our view on many a metaphysical topic. Perhaps it is time to leave this line of reasoning behind us. That quantum behaviour can be understood both as that of a wave or as a particle implies that, on the basic level of "physical" reality, apparent opposites melt together. Perhaps we can indeed have our cake and eat it, much as we can be both human and soul. We need not have life on this side of death and a similarly singular existence on the other side, but rather a multitude, all related in ways we cannot grasp from this particular perspective. Even such terms as good and evil may be inventions of our own, rather than reflections of a natural or divine ethical order. After all, it is that which challenges us that causes us to grow, and there is often more to be learned from situations caused by "evil" as they tend to test our limits and tax our character far more than "good" ones. Good or evil tends to be a question of perspective in human conflicts, much as these concepts themselves would seem to rise from the human perspective.

This does not mean that ethical questions lack significance. To the contrary, there is clearly a purpose to life in the development of spirit, a development that is fully dependent on our thoughts, intentions and actions. To oversimplify: that which furthers spiritual development in ourselves and in others could well correspond to "good," whereas that which hinders development might be described as less good. (I am consciously avoiding the term "evil" because the very word compels us to act judgementally which tends to block any opportunity to learn.) To add to the contradiction, it is possible to act in a way that does not further one's own development but might further someone else's. For example, we might cause someone unnecessary pain by not acting responsibly or out of compassion; this might hinder the development of our spirit and thus be something "bad" from our perspective. On the other hand, the person who is caused pain may well benefit from this if he or she deals with it in a way that furthers the development of spirit, which makes it something "good." This would mean that there is real, if subjective, base for morality even if it does not translate in any simple way into the rules of the objective, physical world.

THE ETHICS OF SPIRIT

One question this model answers quite satisfactorily, I think, is the old metaphysical paradox: If God is good and all-powerful, how can there be so much evil in the world?

If the world is a school for spirits that take on human form and act out of free will, much of what we see as "evil" may serve to teach the spirit valuable lessons; and much of that we consider to be "bad" is caused not by God but by human beings. The world is fully our responsibility—given to us for our own benefit—but the basic rule is one of free will and human autonomy. As spirits we choose the Earth-experience, realising that it is not likely to be a bed of roses and realising that neither God nor any other "higher" being is going to save us from our own choices and our pain because this would defeat the purpose of coming here. Pain is as much a part of the physical world and the physical experience as anything else, but whatever fate befalls our bodies need not affect our souls. The world is simply a place where "bad" things happen, most often directly or indirectly caused by humans, and this is the purpose of Earth. More importantly, it is also a place where "good" things happen and, since there is no one but our self to impel us to do good things, they should be considered all the more beautiful, remarkable and triumphant. In the world of spirits, love and compassion might be the norm which souls act out of; on Earth this would not currently seem to be the case. This is one reason why life as a human can be so rewarding despite all the suffering. If we as spirits all choose the Earth-experience in order to grow, and though from our human perspective it may be tempting to look at the world and see a lot of "evil," this has little to do with the Source or God being all-powerful and good. If there is pain in the world, it is caused by our souls' being confined to physical bodies with physical needs as they learn and strive towards greater perfection.

So is there a spiritual ethic which is the same for all humans? This strikes me as likely, though that ethic is probably concerned more with intent and development—with will—than any actual dictation of correct actions (such as Kant's categorical imperative, to mention but one example). We are all capable of learning from our mistakes, which means that even acting "incorrectly" may well serve a purpose. This, however, demands that we take responsibility for what we do so that our mistakes do not go unchecked and thus turn into failures, into wasted opportunities. To forgive the unrepentant is like painting on the surface of water, as the ancient Chinese saying goes, yet we owe it only to ourselves to provide a more stable canvas.

If we come to Earth to learn, then learning might be a good attitude to take in relating to both the outside world and to our selves—*res cogitans* and *res extensa*. Why do we act the way we do and feel the way we feel? To understand and learn from understanding, we will probably benefit from an open mind more than anything else. Our fears are especially important to acknowledge and even embrace, as they will invariably point to something in us which we need to deal with. That which we cannot control—be it fear or desire, repelling or attracting—will invariably come to control us. We learn more by being open-minded and compassionate than by being judgmental and fearful. Know thyself is both the beacon and the path of the mystic, and so we should pay attention to our feelings—pleasant and unpleasant alike—as they will point to the truths of our souls. Whatever the subjective, spiritual ethic may be, it is up to us to try to find it in our selves.

In dealing with other people, most religions and philosophies seem to agree that compassion and respect for the autonomy of the other is of central importance. Indeed, if we cared for our fellow humans to the degree that we care for ourselves, then our world would no doubt be in better shape. Punishing others for their wrongdoings seems a rather futile endeavour, as punishment rarely teaches anyone to appreciate in what way they have acted wrong, and seems more motivated by a need to avenge oneself than to actually learn anything from what has come to pass. Gaining understanding into self and the world seems to be the whole purpose of life, and one that should be applied in all cases. From this perspective, capital punishment in particular seems a rather odd device for administering justice, as the soul of a killer will no more disappear than the soul of a saint. Better to try to show those who err what they have done so they can start dealing with some of their own issues before death. For those who feel they have be mistreated in some way, the challenge is to deal with what has happened, to resolve any lingering issues and to become complete with it, in order to let go of it. Being unable to let go of what takes place in the physical world seems to lead to its own pitfalls, as many of the reincarnation cases investigated by Dr. Stevenson seem to imply. And, as stated earlier, what we do not deal with during this life we will have to deal with later, elsewhere or in future lives. Pushing others down to elevate oneself, to feel better than or superior to the other person, is unfortunately a common game played among humans, but it is one played at the peril of arrested development. Arguably, the greatest souls to walk this Earth in human guise have always been unassuming, gentle, insightful, open and compassionate. A human being is pure potential, and we are given the freedom of choice to do with that potential what we see fit or deem appropriate.

There are any number of ethical points to be made from the metaphysical model argued here, but these deserve a book of their own. It is sufficient to say that if we embrace the notion of an eternal and developing spirit, living many lives apart from the current one, most of our ethical considerations can be seen in a new light. In fact, much of life appears different when we look at it from a spiritual rather than a human point of view.

BEING HUMAN AND SPIRIT

Being human, then, is not the same as being purely spirit. Rather it involves placing the spiritual in a physical form and forcing it to deal with physical needs—all in the name of spiritual development. Nevertheless, fitting eternal beings into temporal bodies is bound to lead to some problems, which is the main reason there is so much unnecessary suffering on Earth. In dealing with the often overpowering physical world that fills our senses, we tend to forget the spiritual aspects which are always present below the stormy surface of physical life. Sometimes we go so far as to deny the existence of any spirit whatsoever. This is quite understandable, springing from the nature of the physical as it does. Life is stressful and taxes our energy; the vast majority of people in every era has had to struggle to survive. In the spiritual, in life between life, we have no need for such things as food or sleep or shelter in order to survive, or at least not in the sense we do in the physical. Physical life is, simply put, tough. What we need is a shift in attitude about the physical world, our bodies and even our lives. We are not our bodies—they are merely our home away from home—and, as such, they should be treated with love and respect. Neither are we our current personalities, though this might seem a very strange notion indeed. Rather, our consciousness is a point of reference, an origin within the greater origin that is our soul. Perhaps life could be seen as is a battle between ego and self: our ego being temporal and focussed on survival, whereas our self is eternal and focussed on understanding and development. When we speak of appealing to someone's better nature, it is the self we are referring to—that which can rise above our physical needs.

It seems wise not to attach oneself too vigorously to the physical. Physical things are temporal in nature—they simply do not last—and so pose a problem for that in us which is eternal. All owning is a two-way relationship, one where both parties share an equal power over each other; that which we own—or believe we own—does, in fact, own us to an equal degree as we give it that power. As humans we seem bent on owning things, even things such as youth or beauty that cannot be owned for very long; yet we often cling to these for ridiculous lengths of time. We seem to chase youth, wealth and other temporal pleasures much like children chasing toys and, in this process, we find little time to develop our minds, to learn, to gain insight and wisdom, to grow as spirits. The focus on the temporal side of our nature, despite the very futility of it, is probably the greatest pitfall for spirits in human form. We cannot stay young and strong and healthy forever—we must eventually age and grow frail. Indeed, this strikes me as part of the purpose of physical life: to experience the full range of human life with all its inevitable change, something that cannot be experienced in spirit. In attempting to stall it, to experience only part of it, we experience none of it to the fullness that we otherwise might have.

The best attitude is probably to look at the physical as a process rather than a fixed state. An attitude through which we view life and all of its more pleasant physical aspects (such as youth, health and good fortune) as something that is with us for a while, rather than something that belongs to us or defines us. It is how we relate to the physical and what comes to pass here that shapes us, not the fleeting possessions and happenings of objective reality itself. It is not the thing-as-such that is important, but how we relate to it, how we deal with it. We shape our spirits through our attitudes, because these are who we truly are. Though we may be divided in the sense that we are partly temporal in nature and partly eternal in essence, the eternal still builds on the temporal to further itself. Wherever and whatever else we might be, we are foremost here-and-now, and this is where we must create that which we wish to become.

BEYOND DEATH

The destination of our spirit as it leaves the body for the final time is well defined in most religious doctrines—well defined in the sense that a destination of some kind is given, not in the sense that this destination is described in any great detail. As should be evident by now, I believe that there are many possible destinations for our souls; which one we reach depends on the shape of our minds upon death. If our minds are in a state of anger and frustration, we are likely to be drawn to other souls in this state until we manage to separate ourselves from them and proceed to our true home in the spiritual. If our minds are obsessed with some physical aspect of life, we are likely to be drawn to souls with the same obsession, both in and out of human form. If our minds cannot comprehend that we have actually died, we'll probably hang around friends and relatives in a state of confusion, watching them live on and grow older. Eventually these souls will find their way home, sometimes with help and sometimes on their own.[2] I believe it is these groups in particular that explain such phenomena as ghosts, poltergeists and such unfriendly entities that one might mistake for demons when attempting spirit contact. If humans can get lost during life in their struggle for power over others, through abuse and dominance, is it such a stretch of the imagination to assume that this would continue beyond death? Indeed, the demonic and abusive ravings we hear about from people who innocently attempt such parlour games as ouija boards may be the venting of aggression by frustrated spirits stuck between this life and the next. This is, if nothing else, a far less intimidating alternative than the demons and other evil entities of the spiritual world of popular lore. There are no demons, only confused souls/minds that have lost their bodies and their way.

As we move out and away from the physical, we will probably find less horrifying realms than those populated by the closest, most frustrated minds, yet still find spirits that need different kinds of "debriefing" to get away from their particular expectations of the afterlife, their particular mindset. My guess is that these "waiting rooms" of intermediate existence—to make use of a familiar concept—will be primarily filled with minds bent towards one particular religious afterlife expectation or another. As these souls let go of their narrow beliefs and realise that they are merely arrested on a path of spiritual development, they too will be free to move on, to return home.

Home, then, is our particular learning group or level within the spiritual—where we reside when not physically incarnated in one form or another. Here we find old friends and soulmates, teachers and coaches, and others we have known since the origin of our spiritual individuality. This, however, is not our final destination, but rather the central path of development that eventually leads to that final destination: the Source.

Our belief will shape the path of our destiny, but perhaps it ultimately does not matter what we believe if our Source is indeed also our destiny. What is of importance, as I pointed out at the beginning of this book, is that we as humans give our minds and our spiritual development serious consideration—that we make our souls a priority. It seems unlikely that our Earth will suffer us much longer, and even though our spirits are likely to survive whatever happens to our human habitat, it would be a shame not to make a serious effort to improve things. This could be accomplished virtually overnight if everybody would take the spiritual as seriously as the physical, and see the eternal through the delusion of the temporal.

I would like to end this book on that note and leave you with this thought:

Imagine yourself Beyond Death looking back on this, your past life, and ask yourself what kind of conduct would please you as a spirit? What personal challenges met, fears overcome, actions taken and deeds done would make you proud?

In answering this question and moving on through life with that answer always present in your heart, you will have unlocked the secret of spirit and the purpose of your life.

NOTES

CHAPTER 1: A MATTER OF SPIRIT

[1] In the spirit of honesty I should confess that this rather brilliant analogy is not my own, but was related to me by my good friend Sinclair Andersen some years ago as we were discussing the nature of reincarnation. It would serve my own spirit little to take credit for this, though I doubt that he would mind.

CHAPTER 2: CONSCIOUSNESS

[1] This theme is explored in an attainable way in *Darwin's Black Box* by Michael J. Behe.

[2] See *Quantum Questions*, edited by Ken Wilber, Shambhala 1985, for an overview of the mystical writings of several prominent quantum physicists of the past century.

[3] *The Self-Aware Universe* by Amit Goswami, Ph.D., argues this theme, as do several of Gary Zukav's books, to mention a few.

[4] This process is eloquently described in Fred Alan Wolf's *The Dreaming Universe* and in a number of other publications, including Benjamin Libet's original paper *Sensory Referral* from 1979.

[5] The Cartesian Cut refers to the border between *res cogitans* and *res extensa*, the interface between our inner world and that which exists "outside" or "objectively."

CHAPTER 3: MIND OVER MATTER

[1] *The Conscious Universe*, Dean Radin, Ph.D., HarperEdge (p. 128).

[2] The PEAR programme is described in great detail in *Margins of Reality* by Robert G. Jahn and Brenda J. Dunne, and is recommended reading for anyone with a deeper practical and theoretical interest in the topic.

[3] *Margins of Reality*, Robert G. Jahn and Brenda J. Dunne (p. 90).

[4] *The Conscious Universe*, Radin (p. 140).

[5] *The Conscious Universe*, Radin (p. 133).

[6] *The Conscious Universe*, Radin (p. 155).

[7] *The Conscious Universe,* Radin (p. 153).

[8] *The Conscious Universe,* Radin (p. 152).

[9] One such example is the rather humorously titled study "Psychokinetic Action of Young Chicks on the Path of An Illuminated Source" undertaken by René Peoc'h. In this study young chicks (as in poultry) proved able to influence the random behaviour of an illuminated robot in a darkened room, drawing it closer to their section of the room compared to its movements when no chicks were present.

[10] *The Conscious Universe,* Radin (p. 160).

[11] This notion is developed by Amit Goswami in his book *The Self-Aware Universe.*

[12] *The Conscious Universe,* Radin (p. 162).

[13] *The Conscious Universe,* Radin (p. 171).

[14] *The Conscious Universe,* Radin (p. 144).

CHAPTER 4: FORCE OF LIFE

[1] *Miracles of Mind,* Russel Targ and Jane Katra, Ph.D. (p. 195), New World Library 1998.

[2] *Miracles of Mind,* Targ/Katra.

[3] *The Conscious Universe,* Radin, (p. 151).

[4] *Miracles of Mind,* Targ/Katra (p. 217).

[5] *Miracles of Mind,* Targ/Katra (p. 217).

[6] See *The Heart of the Mind* (New World Library 1999) by Jane Katra and Russel Targ, as well as "A Prayer Before Dying" (*Wired* magazine, issue 10, December 2002) by Po Bronson.

[7] *Miracles of Mind,* Targ/Katra, (p. 109)

[8] *Miracles of Mind,* Targ/Katra, (p. 109).

[9] *Miracles of Mind,* Targ/Katra, (p. 199).

[10] *Miracles of Mind,* Targ/Katra, (p. 110).

CHAPTER 5: GREEN-GREY MATTER

[1] From an Interview with Cleve Backster published in *The Sun,* July 1997.

[2] *The Secret Life of Cells,* Robert B. Stone, Ph.D. 1989.

[3] *A New Science of Life,* Rupert Sheldrake, Park Street Press (1995 ed.)

[4] See *Dogs That Know When Their Owners Are Coming Home: and Other Unexplained Powers of Animals* by Rupert Sheldrake.

[5] *The Quantum Self,* Danah Zohar, Flamingo 1991.

CHAPTER 6: EXPANDING MINDS

[1] *The Conscious Universe,* Radin (p. 74).

[2] *The Conscious Universe,* Radin (p. 84).

3 Remote viewing is explored in *The Conscious Universe, Miracles of Mind, & Margins of Reality*, and several other publications listed under recommended reading at the end of this book.

4 *The Conscious Universe*, Radin (p. 194).

5 *The Conscious Universe*, Radin (p. 101).

CHAPTER 7: THE BRIGHTER SIDE OF LIFE

1 See *After the Light: What I Discovered on the Other Side of Life That Can Change Your World*, Kimberly Clark Sharp, New York: William Morrow 1995.

2 *Journal of Near-Death Studies*, summer of 1993 issue.

3 *Mindsight: Near-Death and Out-of-Body Experiences in the Blind* by Kenneth Ring and Sharon Cooper, The William James Center for Consciousness Studies 1999.

4 This information comes from the author's own website (www.melvinmorse.com).

5 Again from the website (www.melvinmorse.com).

6 *Light and Death: One Doctor's Fascinating Account of Near-Death Experiences*, Michael Sabom M.D. Zondervan 1998.

7 *History of Western Philosophy*, Bertrand Russell, (p. 462) Routledge (1993 ed.)

CHAPTER 8: SPIRITS ON THE REBOUND

1 *Where Reincarnation and Biology Intersect*, Ian Stevenson, M.D. (p. 78–80).

2 *Where Reincarnation and Biology Intersect*, Ian Stevenson, M.D. (p. 137).

3 *The Dreaming Universe*, Fred Alan Wolf Ph.D., Touchstone Books 1994.

4 *Where Reincarnation and Biology Intersect*, Stevenson (p. 133).

5 *Where Reincarnation and Biology Intersect*, Ian Stevenson M.D. (p. 111), Praeger 1997.

6 Though the ability to speak a language one is not supposed to have any knowledge of is not a feature reported in Stevenson's *Where Reincarnation and Biology Intersect*, cases of Xenoglossy are nevertheless discussed in *Unlearned Languages: New Studies in Xenoglossy* (University Press of Virginia, June 1984) by the same author as well as by other researchers such as Dr. Whitton in *Life Between Life* and Dr. Brian Weiss in *Message from the Masters*.

7 There are a number of interesting books that describe an abundance of instances where patients use past-life experiences for therapeutic purposes. Since they are, strictly speaking, anecdotal rather than empirical, I have not included references to them in this book, but have provided a list of the books on the subject that I have found the most interesting. See Recommended Further Reading at the end of this book.

CHAPTER 9: CONCLUDING CONSCIOUSNESS

[1] Though reincarnation generally seems to take place not too long after the death of the previous personality, Dr. Stevenson reports at least a few cases where several years would appear to have passed by between the two occurrences (death and birth).

[2] This is not always the case as some people become more rigorous in their beliefs, as Dr. Michael Sabom reports in *Light and Death: One Doctor's Fascinating Account of Near-Death Experiences*, Zondervan 1998.

[3] See *The Conscious Universe*, Radin.

[4] For more information visit the institute on the web at www.monroe-inst.com.

[5] The Lucidity Institute at www.lucidity.com has more information about such techniques, and their objectives.

[6] *The Conscious Universe* Dean Radin.

[7] Several psychologists, researchers and hypnotherapists testify to this effect. Among the more popular documentation of this is *Journey of Souls* by Michael Newton Ph.D., Llewellyn Publications 1998, and others listed under recommended reading at the end of this book.

[8] The Conscious Universe, Radin (p. 201).

[9] One such example is hemisphere synchronisation as developed by *The Monroe Institute*.

[10] *Dying to Live*, Susan Blackmore (p 195).

CHAPTER 10: THE GREAT MYSTERY

[1] *Journey of Souls*, Newton.

[2] Interestingly enough, the *Monroe Institute* has a graduate program known as *Lifeline* where people in out-of-body mode attempt to help such souls find their way "home."

RECOMMENDED READING

For the benefit of those readers that are intrigued by the research referred to in this book, I've included a list of those sources that were particularly helpful.

Of the many publications dealing with non-local consciousness and its interaction with the physical world, the excellent book *The Conscious Universe* (HarperSanFrancisco 1997) by Dean Radin, Ph.D. is the most comprehensive and encompassing work.

Miracles of the Mind (New World Library 1998) by Russel Targ and Jane Katra, Ph.D. is another highly recommended book, dealing in great detail with non-local consciousness and healing. See also *The Heart of the Mind* (New World Library, 1999) by the same authors.

Mind Trek (Hampton Roads Publishing Company 1997) by Joseph McMoneagle deals with his personal experience of remote viewing and related subjects, and *Remote Viewing Secrets* (Hampton Roads Publishing Company 2000), by the same author, focuses on the techniques of Remote Viewing as such.

Margins of Reality (Harcourt Brace 1987) by Robert G. Jahn (Prof. Aerospace Science) and Brenda J. Dunne (manager of PEAR laboratory) deals in great detail with the Princeton Engineering Anomalies Research programme into the interaction between the human mind and physical devices.

Psychic Connections (Delacorte Press 1995) by Lois Duncan and William Roll, Ph.D. deals with a wide variety of phenomena and their practical applications in a descriptive way.

Cleve Backster's research into primary perception is dealt with in *The Secret Life of Plants* by Peter Tomkins & Christopher O'Bird

(HarperCollins 1989) and *The Secret Life of Cells* by Robert B. Stone, Ph.D. (Schiffer Publishing 1989).

Another interesting publication dealing with biology and the evolution of form is *A New Science of Life* by Rupert Sheldrake, Ph.D., and the more directly relevant *Dogs That Know When Their Owners Are Coming Home* (Three Rivers Press 1999) by the same author, which contains a number of studies into telepathic and precognitive abilities among animals.

There are a number of books dealing with the Near Death Experience, though the following recent books are most relevant: *Light and Death* (Zondervan Publishing House 1998) by Michael Sabom, M.D. and *Mindsight* (The William James Centre for Consciousness Studies 1999) by Kenneth Ring, M.D. and Sharon Cooper.

The evidence provided in the chapter on reincarnation originates almost entirely from the fascinating book *Where Reincarnation and Biology Intersect* (Praeger Publishers 1997) by Ian Stevenson, M.D.

For those interested in the more spiritual and philosophical aspects of this book, rather than or in addition to, the purely scientific, I recommend the following books:

Far Journey (Main Street Books 1987) and *Ultimate Journey* (Main Street Books 1996) by Robert A. Monroe, which deal with experiments and experiences of consciousness separated from the body. Eloquently written and thought-provoking. *Cosmic Journeys* (Hampton Roads Publishing Company 1999) by Rosalind A. McKnight has a similar theme, as it deals with the author's experiences over many years at the Monroe Institute. Similarily, Bruce Moen, also associated with the Monroe Institute, has written several books on the topic, under the collective name *Exploring the Afterlife* Series, also published by Hampton Roads Publishing Company, that are of interest, especially the first three books.

For those interested in regression hypnosis and Transpersonal Psychology there are many interesting sources. *Journey of Souls* (Llewellyn Worldwide 1994) by Michael Newton, Ph.D. deals with the author's studies of life as a spirit between lives using hypnosis and regression techniques. These cases are particularly compelling as so many subjects report similar experiences as "spirits." The theme is developed further in *Destiny of Souls* (Llewellyn Worldwide 2000) by the same author. Past life experience and practical use of reincarnation therapy is described in *Past Life Recovery* (Ashgrove Press Limited 1991) by Ingrid Vallieres, as well as in *Only Love Is Real* (Warner Books, 1997) and *Many Lives, Many Masters* (Warner Books, 1994) by Brian Weiss, M.D. *Other Lives, Other Selves* (Bantam-Doubleday-Dell, 1988) by Roger J. Woolger is another excellent example of transpersonal psychology, as is *The Holotropic Mind* (HarperSanFrancisco 1993) by Stanislaf Grof, M.D. and Hal Zina Bennett.

Several interesting books deal with the fascinating world of sub-atomic physics, the following are but a few of those that are both accessible and worth reading:

The Dreaming Universe (Touchstone Books 1994) by Fred Alan Wolf, Ph.D. is nothing less than a completely new hypothesis as to why we dream. It deals with a great many aspects of dreaming, non-local consciousness, and quantum axioms, and is well worth reading. *The Self Aware Universe* (Jeremy T. Tarcher/Putnam 1993) by Amit Goswami, Ph.D. with Richard E. Reed and Maggie Goswami, develops the notion that consciousness rather than matter is the stuff of creation, and also comes highly recommended. *The Quantum Self* (Flamingo 1991) by Dana Zohar, Ph.D. concerns the sense of self from a quantum perspective. Highly readable and thought provoking, as well as a good introduction to quantum physics. *Quantum Mystics* (Shambala 1985) edited by Ken Wilber is a collection of essays from all the great quantum physicists of the last century, dealing with the mystical implications of their discipline, such as the existence of spirit.